Dare to
Commit
Say *Yes* in a World of **Maybe**

JAMES TORRENS, SJ

Liguori

ONE LIGUORI DRIVE
LIGUORI MO 63057-9999

Imprimi Potest:
Thomas D. Picton, C.Ss.R.
Provincial, Denver Province
The Redemptorists

Published by Liguori Publications
Liguori, Missouri
To order, call 800-325-9521
www.liguori.org

Library of Congress Cataloging-in-Publication Data

Torrens, James, 1930-
  Dare to commit : say yes in a world of maybe / James Torrens. — 1st ed.
    p. cm.
  ISBN 978-0-7648-1874-5
  1. Christian life—Catholic authors. 2. Commitment (Psychology)—Religious
aspects—Catholic Church. 3. Torrens, James, 1930- I. Title.
  BX2350.3.T67 2010
  241'.4—dc22
                                                              2009047070

Liguori Publications, a nonprofit corporation, is an apostolate of the Redemptorists. To learn more about the Redemptorists, visit Redemptorists.com.

Printed in the United States of America
14 13 12 11 10   5 4 3 2 1

First edition

CONTENTS

INTRODUCTION

It is high time to speak of commitment, that is to say, of giving oneself to something or someone long-term and then holding on. That takes determination, a sense of what is truly worthwhile, self-discipline, generosity. It takes good examples to give us heart. I say it is high time, because the ambience now is one of non-commitment. When it comes to making and holding to promises, the world fosters discouragement.

My own attention to this topic has grown. When I started teaching college in the '70s and was living among the students, I watched them sign up with enthusiasm for some excursion or activity. But when the date arrived, half would fail to show up. Something better or more pressing had popped up on their screen. This was strange to me, on whom it had been inculcated while growing up that if you give your word, you keep it, cost what that may. In the not entirely mythical tradition of the West, you shake on something, and that seals it. There may be nothing down on paper, but there is no welching. How laughable this sounds now, which shows how far downhill we have gone.

I remember being shocked, at this same Catholic college, that graduates of the business school would accept scholarships from some company for advanced study or would enter their training program with every intention of jumping to something better as soon as it appeared. No commitment felt to the sponsor. That's just the way it is done, I was told. Ethics seemed to play no role. One must add, in the interests of fairness, that so many big companies reneging on loyalty to their long-time servants has weakened their own cause.

The divorce rate is notorious among us. I have no idea how high it is among those whose weddings, as a priest, I have solemnized, but I hope and pray it is below the norm. What has come closer to me is the departure from religious life and priesthood of men and women I have liked and admired, some early on, some after advanced studies, some after many years in the life and service. I try to be appreciative for the years and energy they have given to this call, but I have to acknowledge lingering regret.

A retreat master, Dean Brackley, SJ, put it to us Jesuits recently that we are in a time of temporary vocation; permanent commitment is little valued. He referred to a commitment phobia. We don't want to close any door behind us. Then he said, "Guys, I want to count on you being there with me."

The change of climate is captured for me in an episode of the late '60s, when I was in graduate school at the University of Michigan. Celebrating its sesquicentennial, the school had a series of panels with distinguished speakers. Among them was John Courtney Murray, the Jesuit who had so effectively written about religious freedom and church and state relations at the cost of criticism and strictures from his own church. At lunch with us Jesuit students, he wondered aloud at so many of our fellows who were giving up the ship, as it seemed, because of lesser disappointments and setbacks. He and his colleague, Father Gustave Weigel, had puzzled over this phenomenon.

A host of complexities and considerations belong in this picture. In the case of religious women, for example, there must be sensitivity to all the factors that depleted their numbers during the post-Vatican era. We rely on historians from among them to do that. Each story has unique elements, but the pre-Vatican II era bears a large share of responsibility.

My concern with commitment in the new millennium found a concrete image recently. Stepping out of a department store in Fresno, California, I fell in behind a young woman whose T-shirt announced, "I'm not the commitment type." She and the young man with her were not sophisticates or hipsters, but young Latinos, part of the crowd, displaying a contemporary sentiment.

It is hard not to sympathize with a person who balks at commitment these days, who, for example, has fended off marriage for years. There is a lot at stake. I think about the old conversation between the hen and the pig. The hen is boasting about her daily contributions to men's and women's health, the many eggs she provides. The pig responds: "That's well and good for you, all those contributions. Things are more serious for me. I have to make a commitment." The self of the pig will disappear in the process.

Looked at one way, the disappearance of the self is lamentable, says Margaret Guenther, speaking of women and spiritual direction. "By over-zealousness in their obligations toward others, especially husbands and children, and a corresponding neglect of themselves, women manage to avoid inner growth" (*Holy Listening*, 129). In other words, there has to be a self in the first place. But in a deeper sense, the yielding up of self—"careless abandon," as Guenther puts it—is the goal of the spiritual journey, transformation in God. What a lot of discerning of spirits is called for!

Years ago, when I was still learning Spanish and taking part in an immersion program in Mexico City, I was stopped short by a poster in our conference room. It said: "El secreto de la vida es el compromiso." *What?* I said to myself. *The secret of life is compromise?* But I was far off target. "Compromiso" in Spanish means an agreement you intend to fulfill. It means you have said "yes" to meeting someone somewhere at three o'clock, for instance.

More widely, it refers to a spirit of dedication, for example, the athlete with a rigorous schedule of practice. The secret of life is commitment. That is more like it. Much more has to be said—about maturity, a wise process of decision, widening and deepening of perspective and motives—but that is what it comes down to. The secret of life is commitment.

My thoughts these days keep coming back to a classmate of mine, Chrisologue Mahame, from theology school in 1958 through 1962, in Louvain, Belgium. We were ordained together in 1961. Chrisologue, a Tutsi, was the very first Rwandan to enter the Jesuits. I cannot begin to appreciate what a big leap that must have been.

I knew Mahame in Belgium as very diligent at the books, very earnest and soft-spoken. In the following years, more and more, it seems, he became active for harmony among the two peoples of Rwanda, Tutsi, and Hutu. It concerned him deeply. He promoted it, even at high government levels, from a retreat center in the capital, Kigali. But ever since colonial times, resentments had been seething among the Hutus, the ill feeling fed and finally whipped up by radio and other media. In the bloodbath of 1994, Chrisologue and his team were among the first targeted. They had known very well the risk they were taking. No matter, the secret of life is commitment.

1

Commitment Stories

"I Never Thought You'd Make It"

In 1961, at the time of my priestly ordination in Brussels, Belgium, after studies in Louvain, I received a letter from my cousin, John. We had grown up around the block from each other in San Francisco, six months apart in age, and to this day have remained very close. He said to me, in effect, "I must admit, I never thought you'd make it."

That startled me! On what had he based these doubts? My asthma and iffy health? My timorous bent? He could not have known of my tremors before ordination or how much harder my scrupulosity had made all those seminary years. (The very concept of scruples now needs looking up in a dictionary.)

Yet deep down, I never really had any doubts about my life's direction. I had known since the seventh grade that I wanted to be a Jesuit priest like my Uncle Carlo. Through all the headiness and confusion of the 1960s and '70s, and despite some false steps of my own, our Lord kept me close to his heart and true to my original direction. Daniel, the prophet, had it right when he said, "[T]hose who trust in you cannot be put to shame" (3:40).

Born to One's Calling

What a tremendous mystery this all is, the mystery of a calling. Dom Helder Camara, Cardinal of Recife and beloved bishop of the poor in northeastern Brazil, put the case wonderfully in speaking about himself:

> Look, there are those who are born to sing, those who are born to write, those who are born to play soccer, and those who are born to be priests. I was born to be a priest. I started saying so at the age of eight, and certainly not because my parents put the idea in my head. My father was a Mason, and my mother went to church once a year.
>
> I even remember that one day my father got frightened and said: "My son, you're always saying you want to be a priest. But do you know what that means? A priest is someone who doesn't belong to himself, because he belongs to God and to people, someone who must dispense only love and faith and charity."
>
> And I said, "I know. That's why I want to be a priest."

Dom Helder, at this early age, had no inkling that he and his labors would come to epitomize liberation theology in Brazil, and that the churches worldwide would honor him for that. He had no inkling of the hostility he would arouse from exploiters of the poor. He only knew, precociously, that God called him as a priest loud and clear.

The example of Dom Helder Camara lets us know that we use the phrase "one's calling" more lightly than we should. How compelling and mysterious is the call from a divine source, whatever one's mission or direction be. The whole history of the Chosen People in the Bible begins with these compelling words of God to Abraham, son of a settler in Assyria: "Go forth from the land of your kinsfolk and from your father's house to a land that I will show you" (Genesis 12:1). With unquestioning obedience, Abraham embarked with his raggedy entourage into the unknown. Beginning with him and his mysterious vocation, the history of God's providence for his people unfolds. With reason, then, does Saint Paul single out as the Christian paradigm "the faith of Abraham, who is the father of all of us" (Romans 4:16).

The Irresistible Summons

A calling, a vocation of any kind, is truly a summons, an appeal for some generous response. To bring this home to us we have classic examples of appeal and response. Gautama, the Buddha, was drawn by the world's suffering out of his princely cocoon of comforts. Mohammed, thanks to his visions, was impelled out of a narrow village world into the near-Eastern mainstream with his message of submission to the Almighty. The tenor of their lives changed drastically. Among the prophets propelled into denouncing unholy conduct, against all his own instincts, think of Jeremiah, forever famous for his laments. "Whenever I speak, I must cry out, violence and outrage is my message" (20:8). Jeremiah yearned to escape his role, to get out of his commitment. "You duped me, O Lord, and I let myself be duped; you were too strong for me, and you triumphed....I say to myself, I will not mention him, I will speak in his name no more. But then it becomes like fire burning in my heart, imprisoned in my bones; I grow weary holding it in, I cannot endure it" (20:7, 9). Poor man, he did endure it, he did go out and give his people a tongue lashing for their idolatry and neglect of the Law, their heedlessness of God. For his blunt predictions of disaster, he was scourged and put in stocks for mockery and was barely spared death. At the end, however, after the exile to Babylon, Jeremiah was vindicated and his prophecies brightened into a view of Jerusalem restored, in fact, into an announcement of the New Covenant.

When it comes to irresistible summons, think of the Twelve Apostles. They emerge before us as the prime example of following one's star. The one thing we know about their calling—according to Matthew, Mark, and Luke—is that Jesus appealed to them in a commanding way: "Follow me." Period. The sequence is made to seem especially abrupt with the call of Matthew. "[Jesus] saw a man named Matthew sitting at the customs post. He said to him, 'Follow me.' And he got up and followed him" (Matthew 9:9).

Those three Gospels reduce commitment to its bare bones—a strong invitation finding a ready response. We are not told that these young men had heard and watched Jesus, nor that he enthralled them. Only the Gospel of John, in its opening chapter, treats of the process of attraction, without which no response is conceivable. John the Baptist had pointed Jesus out to Andrew and his unnamed companion with the words: "Behold the Lamb of God." Jesus, when they come up to him, inquires: "What are you looking for?" They ask, "Where are you staying?" and he responds, "Come and you will see" (1:38–39). What a lot of language there is in this passage about looking at and looking for. Andrew and his companion do go and see and are quickly convinced that here, in Jesus of Nazareth, they have found what they have most been looking for, the true messenger of God, the Messiah. A chain of enthusiasm surges from Andrew to Peter, thence to Philip, and finally to Nathaniel, by chapter's end.

The stories of apostolic calling and commitment as narrated in the Gospels can help us in two ways. Matthew, Mark, and Luke present the vocation—what God really calls us to—as something radical: "Drop everything and come on." Every genuine calling has to have that quality. Saint John stresses the development of a call, its attraction, its contemplative basis: "Open your eyes and ears. Do you like this? Is it for you?"

Let Your Life Speak

The disciples let themselves be caught entirely. That is the essential feature of a calling. You yield to it. And if it doesn't just hit you and possess you or declare itself little by little and nag at you, go look for it. That is the message of Parker Palmer in his exhortatory book, *Let Your Life Speak: Listening for the Voice of Vocation*. Palmer had labored along the trail of doctoral research and academic ambition at the University of California with little real contentment. It eventually came home to him that this was not his gift or his pleasure (as in the mantra, "Follow your pleasure"). It was not his true desire. In *Let Your Life Speak*, he explains what, at high cost, he came to realize, that he was called to another model of education.

> Vocation at its deepest level is not, "Oh, boy, do I want to go to this strange place where I have to learn a new way to live and where no one, including me, understands what I'm doing." Vocation at its deepest level is, "This is something I can't not do, for reasons I'm unable to explain to anyone else and don't fully understand myself but that are nonetheless compelling" (25).

One's life really begins when one's calling dawns and one's commitment clicks in. The examples above, mostly scriptural, illustrate how that happens. The commitment can be to a hero or admired model; it can be to a cause, to a certain path ahead (perhaps a Way), to a trusted partner.

Many people we know impress us as having found what they are good at, what their gift is, and are simply hitting their stride. In the best of cases, they are committed to what they are engaged in. They would not think of another existence nor of greener pastures. Not everyone, by a long shot, has that luxury. Labor is still grinding for the majority of the human family. Close to home in this country, we have all those who, desperate to escape rural poverty, have hazarded the border crossing from Mexico. Yet the immigrant poor, too—so many of them—commit themselves to the goal of making opportunity available, above all, for their sons or daughters. Through their offspring, by proxy, their journey in a new world will go that much farther.

Looking Back From the Anniversary

Married couples who arrive at the major anniversaries, twenty-fifth and beyond, persuade us most of the time of how committed they are to each other. They have found their calling as spouses. Likely they have found their calling as parents, too—not an untroubled calling most of the time, but one they hold to firmly. To be a good parent is never something that just happens, a habit that one falls into. These are major, absorbing occupations that a man or woman needs to decide on and follow through on, whatever be the crying needs or deviations of the children.

The commitment of marriage, whatever the belief system of the man or woman, involves a major promise: "I will be true to you till death." Among relationships, it is the privileged instance of a long-term mutual project springing from a strong affective bond. Often enough, when the mate dies, the one left behind is desolate; their inner life a kind of baffled groaning. In many Hispanic countries, matrimony includes the ceremony of the lasso, the cord that is tied symbolically around both partners. Much humor has ensued about a mate being "roped" or "tied down," but the ceremony is taken quite seriously as an image of association until death. The strands of the lasso, as it is often designed, compose into a rosary with all the expected segments. The lasso thus speaks of a prayerful binding.

The mutual consent of spouses, in a high percentage of cases, is sealed with a vow. We use the word "vow" pretty widely, as when vowing to accomplish something; and it is often used negatively, as when one vows to get revenge. But at its core, "to vow" means to promise something with God as witness, or, as we say, "with the help of God."

How many times I have witnessed and blessed the exchange of marriage vows. It has never been routine. On the contrary, I think of it as the priest's role at its most serious, with the most at stake for society and church. One fragile human being, just starting on the path to adulthood most of the time, says to the other: "I take you for better or for worse, for richer or poorer, in sickness and in health, until death." Gulp! No wonder so many grooms sweat profusely or fortify themselves with spirits for this moment. No wonder smelling salts are reserved for the bride.

A couple marrying is blissfully unaware of the rough patches ahead. The list of possible crises is endless. It doesn't take a novelist to imagine them, for the people we know offer us ready samples of a road prodigal with big branches and stones. Every so often I get to remembering a brief passage from one of the novels of the 1950s by Bruce Marshall. As two women are leaving church on Sunday morning after Mass, one says to the other, "Wasn't that a lovely sermon that Father gave us today about marriage?" The other one answers, "Yes, it certainly was, and I wish I knew as little about it as he does."

The Joyces, the Lincolns, and Jonathan

Good examples and stories of commitment in human relations hearten us greatly, odd as some of them may be, as in the movie, *Harold and Maude*. The domestic life of James Joyce certainly had its oddities but also a remarkable toughness. The biographers of Joyce, that genius of Irish fiction, have to admit that he owed his sexual initiation to the prostitutes of Dublin. Things changed when he met and fell for an attractive but simple country girl from Galway, Nora Barnacle. He induced her to come live with him, and before long, to leave Ireland with him on his self-imposed exile in Europe. Joyce's father, himself something of a wit, remarked that with that name, "She'll stick with him," and she did.

Joyce was adamant against marriage, though he eventually had to accede to a civil ceremony to give his wife and children legal protection. He often made Nora's life a headache. Whenever the two were distant, she had to endure his raunchy imaginings conveyed by letter, plus who knows what sexual indignities at home, followed often by profuse apology. Strangest of men he may well have been, but he was also hers. She bore him two children, one of whom, their daughter Lucia, inherited her mother's and father's poor eyesight and eventually verged into mental illness. Life for the Joyces had frequent changes of address—Trieste, Switzerland, Paris. Nora, as well, had to monitor James's drinking and, in Paris, play hostess to the multiple guests whom Joyce loved to receive in the evenings. Altogether she is one of those background players in literary history whose common sense and strength made an artistic life possible for her spouse.

For another admirable commitment against ferocious odds, we can consider the story of Abraham and Mary Todd Lincoln. Upon Lincoln's election, when they moved into the capital, the establishment gentry and the press, as well, took constant aim at the upstart first lady's florid style and her frank self-expression. Her whole tenure at the White House was shadowed by the storm clouds of the Civil War. Her sprightliness often had to relieve the president's melancholy over the war.

In those pre-antibiotic days, when fevers menaced their three boys, anxiety beset the Lincolns. Their youngest and dearest,

Willie, died in the White House. If Mary was prone afterwards to take the two remaining sons out of Washington into New England or elsewhere, who could blame her? Through all of this time, the president's attachment to his wife, his concern for her and his need of her company, was evident to everyone. Lincoln's death at Ford's Theater on Good Friday, on an evening out that he undertook for her sake, devastated Mary and partially unhinged her. In retrospect, if the war years made Lincoln shine as national leader at a huge personal cost, they at the same time brought out his best as spouse and father. He lived by his vows a hundred percent.

Burrowing into our Scriptures for astonishing commitment, we go to the artful narratives of The Book of Kings and come upon the story of Jonathan, son of Saul, and the young hero, David (1 Samuel 18—20). We are told, with maximum economy and clarity, "Jonathan entered into a bond with David, because he loved him as himself. Jonathan divested himself of the mantle he was wearing and gave it to David, along with his military dress, and his sword, his bow and his belt" (18:3–4). Thus armed, David succeeded in every mission that Saul gave him.

When Saul turned against David, Jonathan protected him, both by spying for David and by his pleas for David to his father. When the dispraise of David sounded, "Jonathan sprang up from the table in great anger...for he was grieved on David's account, since his father had railed against him" (20:34). Saul is understandably angry that his son has, in effect, given up his claim to the kingdom in favor of the son of Jesse. There is a touching moment of David and Jonathan's farewell, before David takes flight. "They kissed each other and wept aloud together" (20:41). Jonathan concludes: "The Lord shall be between you and me, and between your posterity and mine forever" (20:42). It is their last encounter. Jonathan is destined to die soon with his father, but his commitment remains there in the Bible, shining.

Keeping the Call Fresh

Whatever calling one is gifted with—the call to be a faithful friend, the call to be a reliable workman, the call of public service, the call of a devoted spouse, the call to help others in need, the call of art—it is intended to be long-term. That means staying in condition and always having it in the back of one's mind. A calling invites a commitment. The commitment means, "Yes, I am ready to take this seriously." Someone I know once asked Van Cliburn, the pianist, how much he practiced in the course of a day. We have here someone of proven ability at the highest level and a demanding but familiar schedule. What is he going to answer? "Nine hours a day," was Cliburn's answer.

We don't have to be tense about commitment; tension cannot hold up very long. We can be intense about it, however, always on our toes. The Swiss doctor and mystic, Adrienne von Speyr, has something arresting to say about the continuing urgency of the divine call, whatever be its actual content. She reminds us that a vow, a commitment, or a calling is never something of the past, but an actual presence. We know all about the eucharistic presence, she says:

> But we are less ready to believe that, once his call has been heard and answered, it continues to echo in our lives, that it never ceases to do so, that the word must never become a resting-place. The call should be as important to us as the most serious concerns of the Church—both our own call and that of others. We must remain, at any cost, in the number of those who keep the call alive in themselves, and we must pray for the grace to do so.

Quoted in *Magnificat*, August 5, 2008

The phenomenon of men—males, specifically—walking away from their family commitments has been all too prevalent over the last fifty years. In 1990, a group of Evangelical Protestants, at the urging of the ex-football coach of the University of Colorado, Bill McCartney, began huddling for a counter strategy—assemble men all over the country so as to bolster them and keep them true to their Christian motivation. The movement, non-denominational in scope, communicates its focus in the title, Promise Keepers.

McCartney envisioned filling the Denver stadium, Folsom Field, with its capacity of fifty thousand for a yearly conference. By their third year, 1993, he and his associates and staff had reached this goal. The yearly assemblies then began to multiply in other locales and culminated on the National Mall in 1996 with a million participants. Thereafter, Promise Keepers went a bit quieter but kept up its events in stadiums and arenas and its flow of publications and videos. In September 2008, Bill McCartney came out of retirement to lead the attempt at a second spring for the movement.

In a secular age such as ours, a time of spiritual and cultural complexity and bafflement, Promise Keepers has a huge challenge to follow up their mass gatherings with small, regular ones and with instruction, counsel, and encouragement to individuals. The purpose of including the Promise Keepers here, at the end of examples and stories of commitment past and present, is to describe a vigorous effort to stir commitment on a broad front and to do so among many who notably sloughed off.

The best place to close this survey of the field, this gallery of samples from a broad spectrum of commitments, should probably be the attitude openly fostered in the Psalms. "I will pay my vows to the Lord in the presence of all his people, / In the courts of the house of the Lord, in your midst, O Jerusalem" (Psalm 116:18–19). If we could only be up to that!

2

Elements of Commitment

Clearing Up an Opaque Concept

To the philosophically minded, the topic or the concept of commitment must seem vague and amorphous, pretty slippery. For instance, can my agreement to have lunch next week with an old childhood friend be called a commitment? And if I say yes to meeting with someone I find disagreeable, is that a commitment? How about announcing a weekend trip to the zoo to my children? What if I have a new job with a Silicon Valley company, and I am trying hard to identify with the company's goals and purposes. Is that a commitment?

I confess to having wandered into this topic of commitment intent on encouraging it and illuminating it, but without very precise terminology. Happily, I stumbled upon a guide through these thickets. He is the moral philosopher Marcel S. Lieberman, author of *Commitment, Value and Moral Realism* (Cambridge Studies in Philosophy, 1998). Lieberman admits readily that commitment has been "an opaque concept" among moral theorists, "about which one could conjecture freely" (194), but he has set himself to remedy this defect.

As is obvious from our first chapter and from the opening paragraph above, "commitment" covers a wide range of actual and possible cases. Lieberman maintains that all these varieties of commitment form a continuum, but claims they can be roughly divided into two types: intention-like commitments and substantive commitments. Substantive commitments concentrate on strong and more sweeping values, the more enduring human goods.

Among the intention-like commitments, Lieberman's most frequent example is language learning, especially if one is not pushed to it by necessity but drawn to it, rather, by personal interest. Another example he gives is of the student determined to complete a college paper over the coming weekend. If a phone call comes on Saturday inviting him or her out, the answer will have to be the familiar one, "No, I've got a paper due on Monday." A research project for such a student can be an even more absorbing and open-ended commitment. Consider also the many jobs in the garden or garage or around the house that spouses commit to as part of their much larger and substantive commitment to one another.

When people these days sit down to count up all they are involved in, they often find themselves over-committed. Whether this stems from eagerness or family complications or whatever, it involves a failure to prioritize, with consequent fatigue and dissipation of energies. Commitments can compete with one another, in which case somebody wins and somebody loses. For example, an Asian woman I know tends the two children of a professional couple who, even at home, are constantly on the cell phone or answering email. Due to the couple's dedication to outside commitments, she is, for all practical purposes, the mother of those children.

I am aware of undertakings in my life which should have been commitments but really were not. In high school, I played clarinet in the R.O.T.C. band, mostly to avoid the drill and the rifles. I did so without much in the way of lessons or practice. This was non-commitment. As a college teacher, decades later, I sang with a community chorale and certainly took part in rehearsals but did not practice much on my own, though I often needed to. Weak commitment, if any.

Substantive Commitment: Case Histories

Substantive commitment is familiar to most of us. I have some good examples close around me. My brother, Paul, fixed his professional sights on medicine years ago in high school. Upon graduating from medical school, he found himself drawn to public health and eventually came to focus on hospital administration and health services. At U.C.L.A., where he still teaches, he developed an executive training program for health administrators in Los Angeles and surrounding counties. In his seventies, though no longer its director, he is still fully active in this program. Public health professionals are a tight fraternity worldwide, a fact which has taken Paul abroad to consult public entities in the Caribbean, Africa, Indonesia, and China. That commitment has marked his life.

My cousin, John, whom I alluded to in Chapter One, is an orthopedist and thus a veteran of emergencies and long working days. Nonetheless, his focus upon his family—his wife, Nancy, and his five children—has always come first, no bones about it. Nancy, he readily admits, deserves the lion's share of the credit, but he has been no reluctant lion himself. Their children, and now their grandchildren, have been the great beneficiaries. A footnote belongs here. Part of John's vigilance consisted in prohibiting television in his house so his children would read. This may have backfired; four of them grew up to be lawyers. The youngest, at long last, followed his father into orthopedics.

One of the priests with whom I now reside is in his mid-seventies and is a prison chaplain part-time and a social activist here in agricultural country, a poor and pretty conservative segment of California. He got the bug for social action, he tells everyone, as a young priest teaching at Loyola High School in Los Angeles, when some of his students urged him to accompany them on inner-city projects. From such chance events do lives often turn one hundred eighty degrees.

Take the similar case of Saint Vincent de Paul. In seventeenth-century France, Monsieur Vincent was a young chaplain to a well-off family with large properties. He was asked to hear the confession of an old peasant close to death. "I was doomed if you hadn't come," the man told him. Vincent, full of ambitions for advancement in the upper echelons of Church and society, was so struck by the crying needs of the peasantry crystallized in this man that it changed his life. He became chaplain to galley slaves, preacher of missions in the countryside, the impelling force behind the Daughters of Charity and founder of his own missionary society devoted to seminary instruction, for example, to the dispelling of ignorance among the clergy.

Marcel Lieberman, for his major example of substantive commitment, chooses the old-time labor activist and socialist pioneer Eugene Debs. Debs contributed enormously to the American labor movement and the rights of women and blacks, at high personal cost and risk, which included stays in jail. Debs was from Terre Haute, Indiana, where, as his biographer Bernard Brommel records, "The very concept of manhood hinged on the ability of any given individual to assume in his localized social group personal responsibility for his deeds."

Debs's concern for the workingman, nonetheless, did not so much derive from the molding given him by his milieu as from his reading of literature and his hard personal experience. His peers at home, he came to discover, had limited perspectives on many issues. He came to a deeper understanding of fundamental values, such as manhood, justice, and dignity, by critically reflecting on them, Lieberman tells us. And "he felt the pull of consistency, publicity [the test of public exposure] and universality on the principles he held."

What Makes for a Commitment

So with Debs before us and other examples that each reader can call to mind, the moment has come to ask, What exactly, among all our mental processes and volitions, is a commitment? The intelligence and the powers of volition both have to enter in. The process can be roughly considered as two-stage. After observation and judgment, we arrive at some determination about what merits doing. Thereupon the free will determines—engages itself strongly—to carry out the action.

Marcel Lieberman gives us a good example of what cannot be called a commitment, what has not reached that stage. "Someone who gives up on a puzzle as soon as it becomes challenging or abandons a plan as soon as it encounters obstacles, is not a person we would describe as being committed." This sentence, when I first read it, brought me up short, because I really enjoy word games, including crossword puzzles. But I know when I pick up the *New York Times* on Saturday and turn to the crossword, that I will get frustrated in no time. I am likely to abandon the Sunday crossword too, tempting though it is for its long, clever, interrelated fill-ins. So I am not committed to something that I do find challenging and enjoy. We all know people who, once they start a crossword, are hooked and will not put it down until completion or exhaustion of all their resources.

Does a commitment admit of exceptions? Lieberman, along the line, introduces the concept of "defeasibility." Situations will arise when we cannot be true to our commitment. Though a person may be strongly anti-war or pro-life, he or she cannot be active on that front all of the time, protesting continually. This does not mean they are reconsidering. My own example is dietary. I avoid red meat for medical reasons and for be-kinder-to-animals reasons. But if I find myself at a dinner party where that is the only main course, I will partake. Another of the priests I live with, however, is a vegan. For him, no circumstance will permit exception. He too has to attend lunches and dinners, but he picks only what answers to his specs and ends up with a lot of big salads. When he shops, everything pretty much has to be marked "organic." Whole Foods, Trader Joe's, and Farmer's Market love to see him coming. So Lieberman is right to say, concerning the defeasibility of commitments, "What counts as an exception to their application will vary depending on what is at stake." For a true vegan, something major is at stake!

Another anecdote suggests itself here. Years ago, in the pretty strict old days, headaches were an occupational hazard for seminary students, including us members of the Society of Jesus. One such Jesuit seminarian, badly afflicted, went to see a doctor who naively told him, "What you need is a vacation from the vows." The doctor may have had in mind dating, free spending, and trips without permission. That would certainly have been a major break in the commitment, a circumstance perhaps canceling the contract ("defeasible" is, after all, a legal term). Vows do not allow of a hiatus.

Commitment Is Stable

Marcel Lieberman very helpfully and, in fact, repeatedly lists the three elements that make up a commitment. It is stable over time, guides action, and plays a role in a person's self-understanding and identity.

First, stability. A commitment of ours will act as a blueprint to continue directing us and impelling us. Any reconsideration reverberates to the center of our psyche, especially with substantive commitments. Lieberman says, "What underwrites the stability of commitment is the stability or continuity of one's self-conception," that is, the idea one has of oneself. Adhering to a commitment gradually becomes a habit, a second nature—a deliberate, not an automatic, habit—something to the forefront of consciousness.

One curious example of stability comes to me almost daily. I once heard that General Augusto Pinochet of Chile took a cold shower every morning. Adherence to cold showers is a trait I can admire, whatever I may otherwise think of the general. I have to confess that every morning now, when showering warm or hot, my mind ruefully turns to the general. I judge myself, by comparison, a poor physical specimen, as he may well have intended.

I am a Catholic priest and have been so for almost fifty years. Priesthood, certainly one of the substantive commitments, calls for stability, mental and occupational. My own ups and downs, attraction to greener grass, times of minor depression, and responsibilities beyond me have put their stress on this commitment. Still, if I kept on questioning whether being a priest has value, I would be in real trouble. I cannot let myself be unsettled by disparagements such as this one that I once heard. Groucho Marx, the waspish comedian, was in a hotel elevator somewhere when a priest happened to enter it. Moved by the encounter, the priest said to him, "Mr. Marx, I want to thank you for all the joy you have brought into people's lives." Groucho answered, "I wish I could say the same for you guys." I have to tell myself, *De te fabula*, in the Latin aphorism that means, "The story is about you." But my conclusion has to be not "Give it all up," but "Brighten up!"

Commitment Guides Action

The second detectable quality of a commitment is that it guides action. A commitment, for example, will generate policies. "I never drink if I have to do the driving." "I always do my daily meditation first thing after getting up." "I always leave my office door open." "I never drive outside San Francisco." My mother uttered that last one in her later years; many non-natives would say just the reverse. The more general commitments behind these policies are not hard to detect. The policies, no doubt, can admit of exceptions—"Just one little glass of wine!"—but not many. With commitments, says Lieberman, there seem to be more occasions when exercising flexibility does, in fact, constitute reconsideration.

A commitment functions as a filter of choices. Certain courses of action are clearly filtered out. The proverbial stop at the bar after work is filtered out by commitment to the family dinner. A golf game or a visit to the hairdresser is filtered out by the report I have to get done pronto. Channel cruising on TV may be filtered out by determination to keep watch over my fantasies. There is an element of rigidity, then, in commitments—especially substantive ones.

Faithfulness to commitment involves discipline, postponed gratification, something we used to call self-sacrifice, even risk. For example, to be committed to law enforcement in Mexico these days is to put one's life in the line of fire. Or in the case of Eugene Debs, his social activism, especially during World War I, left him exposed to hounding by the government as it stretched the Espionage Act of 1917. A few Socialists were lynched in 1917. WWI workers were driven out of some working places. Commitments to honesty and integrity as they have to be exercised in dicey situations in the work force can also be, as Lieberman puts it, "counter-prudential." That by no means rules them out.

The marital commitment is our major example of guided action, words determining one's future course. "I promise to be true to you in good times and in bad, in sickness and in health. I will love you and honor you all the days of my life." Especially when you know that good or bad times can mean richer or poorer, that is a lot to bite off.

Commitment Shapes Our Sense of Identity

The major and crucial thing about commitment, again according to Lieberman but also according to common sense, is that, besides orienting action, it enhances our self-understanding and shapes our sense of identity. That is a theme throughout his book, *Commitment, Value and Moral Realism*. Commitments, or lack of them, make us who we are. Scott Simon, the host of the Saturday morning *Newshour* on National Public Radio, gave an affecting profile of his mother on the "Story Corps" segment of NPR (November 21, 2008), to which he added this coda: "A woman who's had four last names is not shy about commitment." She has not been one to rest easy with widowhood. She has not, despite the death of spouses, let dejection and melancholy take over her life.

A commitment, by its very nature, is about something important to us, something of real value. It can be what Lieberman calls a "personal value," which contrasts with what he calls an "impersonal value," such as environmental action or conservative politics. For example, I myself recognize the need I have to exercise, mainly by a brisk walk, at least every few days. Lieberman would want to know from me whether this connects to some recognizable value that others can recognize, a value that is objective for others as well as subjective for me. I need the awareness that a commitment to exercise captures a certain fact about human nature or the human good, that exercise is salutary, period. Yes, I can tell him. Exercise is worthwhile in itself and has value. I believe that just as firmly as I did in my heyday of jogging.

Lieberman says, "Such a belief results from a process of deliberation and assessment on the part of the agent...which provides (or could provide) a coherent account of why she has this commitment." He adds, "Quite simply, we accept the commitments we do because we believe them to be objectively valuable or worthwhile.... The 'deep rationale' supporting the higher-order norms is that they are 'getting it right,' 'are true,' or 'hit on the facts'" (188).

We need coherent accounts to be able to justify ourselves when questioned or challenged about a given commitment. When our commitments are questioned or even challenged, we need beliefs, evaluative rankings, reasons "that others, though they might not accept them, could at least find intelligible or reasonable." This is by no means a new insight. We find something very germane, very instructive in the New Testament (1 Peter 3:15): "Always be ready to give an explanation to anyone who asks you for a reason for your hope."

Our guide heretofore in the analysis of commitment, Marcel Lieberman, underlines the importance of commitments to our self-understanding in the recourse he has to Charles Taylor, that looming figure among moral philosophers of the late twentieth century.

> Charles Taylor...develops the "profound" sense of self-understanding—a form of self-understanding which enables us to develop coherent stories of our lives and provides us with an orientation according to which we can pursue goals. For Taylor, forming commitments is a necessary part of being a full human agent: it is on the basis of one's commitments that one develops the "frameworks" of meaning which are essential to human agents for making sense of their lives, since such frameworks allow one "to determine from case to case what is good, or valuable, or what ought to be done." (*Commitment, Value, and Moral Realism*, 16.)

We do not go about consciously to build frameworks, I suppose, but we can recognize and give thanks for them when we have them. The chapters immediately to come will explore what a state we find ourselves in when we fail to have such frameworks or when we repudiate them.

How About the Dubious Commitments?

One may well ask at this point whether all these praises of commitment are not terribly naïve. Think of the fierce commitments that are roiling the world, that have become a black hole sapping out the humanity of so many. Think of the militants in Pakistan going on the rampage against hundreds of schools for girls, or the young person strapping on explosives to walk into an ordinary crowd and immolate as many as he or she can. Is not their twisted version of true faith and their image of martyrdom a very model of commitment?

Think also, closer to home, of the Aryan Brotherhood and the Klan and other hellbent watchdogs. In fact, think back into history about the time-honored vendetta, where you pledge yourself to get even for injury of a buddy or family member. With vendettas, the past still lives in the present. Do not all the above qualify as commitments? So must we not sweep into a cocked hat all the praises of commitment?

Marcel Lieberman never poses that question to himself. He does not really have to. None of the above causes, which have thrown religion itself into disrepute and darkened our family history, rate as substantive values. They exclude themselves from a moralist's sense of commitment. They infringe on that most basic human norm, the Golden Rule, whether in its positive or negative form—Do unto others as you would have them do unto you; do not do unto others what you would not like them to do unto you. And clearly the causes and motivations listed above also shrug off the explicit teaching of Jesus about the two great commandments, all-out love of God and love of one's neighbor as of one's self. Harboring the bitterness and harshness and anger that they do, they fail, woefully, the love-of-neighbor test. As to the self understanding they derive from their causes, how narrow that is bound to be. In no way do we want to let this fanaticism or ill will into the tent of commitment.

3

Commitment? I Should Say Not!

Augustine, Not Yet Saint

Remember the young Latina I mentioned in the "Introduction," the one I saw in a mall in Fresno wearing the T-shirt that proclaimed, "I'm not the commitment type"? This piece of clothing and the with-it saying were not of her own making. It had to emerge from some matrix, some milieu where that attitude circulates, humorously or not. This makes me ask: Are there really non-commitment sorts of people or sets of people?

There have always been hedonists, to begin there. According to Saint Luke, one of the last warnings of Jesus, just before his suffering and death, was not to be creatures of appetite and self-interest and lose sight of the divine judgment, the day of the Lord. "Beware that your hearts do not become drowsy from carousing and drunkenness and the anxieties of daily life, and that day catch you by surprise like a trap" (21:34). Augustine of Hippo, as he tells us in his *Confessions*, was one such young man, sexually active even while in urgent pursuit of the truth. He is known for his plaintive prayer, "Lord, give me chastity, but not yet."

The turning point for Augustine, in what he calls his "turbulent delayings" and his final effusion of tears and "miserable exclamations," was when he heard a child's voice from a neighbor house singing, "*Tolle, lege, tolle, lege*" ("Pick up and read, pick up and read"). It was like a child's rhyme, but he could not remember ever having heard it. He concludes "that I was from God himself commanded to open the book [the Bible] and to read that chapter which I should first light upon." The chapter his eyes first lit upon was from Saint Paul to the Romans: "...not in orgies and drunkenness, not in promiscuity and licentiousness, not in rivalry and jealousy. But put on the Lord Jesus Christ, and make no provision for the desires of the flesh" (13:13–14). He goes on to say: "No further would I read; nor needed I." From this moment on, he was resolved. "A light as it were of confidence now darted into my heart, all the darkness of doubting vanished away" (*Loeb Classics, St. Augustine's Confessions, Book VIII*).

The example of Augustine, plaything of impure desires even while in the serious pursuit of truth, has always impressed and fascinated readers of the *Confessions*. He enacted the universal story as described by Saint Paul: "I take delight in the law of God, in my inner self, but I see in my members another principle at war with the law of my mind....Miserable one that I am!" (Romans 7:22–24). He endured intensely and described memorably the battle we all know, of impulse with principle, of selfishness with generosity.

The World of the Wantons

Marcel Lieberman, in his analysis of commitments, reminds us that "commitments as we typically understand them are formed in part as an assurance that we will continue a general course of action even in those times when it is no longer 'fun' to do so." The kind of person incapable of this he calls "a wanton." This he describes as "an agent who lacked the capacity to form second-order volitions," that is to say, one who is unable to carry out effectively any first-order, substantive desires. We can think of the young Augustine, or of Ethel Merman singing, "I'm just a girl who can't say no." Immediate inclinations dominate. For such persons, their desires are not really theirs. Conversion, reform, maturing of such a person would mean returning control of the desires to this particular agent himself or herself. Divine intervention, thanks to the prayers of his mother Monica, did that for Augustine. "Wantons" need a capacity for "second-order volitions," that is, choices that conform to ideals, principles, norms, substantive commitments. The challenge, says Lieberman, is "changing the wanton into a person...one that is not reduced to the field of play for her desires."

The field of play for desires is pretty wide these days! Among all the liberations of the past century, including feminism, perhaps the earliest was the liberation of the libido. An excuse for this opening to sensuality has always been ready at hand: "Let's get rid of Puritanism. Enough of the puritanical!" Like any good excuse, this one had substantial grounds in the close monitoring of conduct, including "the blue laws" that we associate with New England and later came to describe as "Victorian." But moderation, good sense, and honesty went by the boards in exercising this liberation. Films, television, print media, the Internet, ways of dressing and of socializing, now more than ever, foment sexual attraction. What ever happened to the genuine respect for women that feminism was supposed to foster? It's a victim of the sensate age.

One effect of the sensate age, on college campuses at least, has been the "hook-up culture." Simply put, it is pressure towards recreational sex. For many, it is not even recreational, since they do not really enjoy it or approve of it but go along because that's what everybody does and talks about. Donna Freitas, a professor at Saint Michael's College in Vermont, surveyed and interviewed students on the topic for her book, *Sex and the Soul: Juggling Sexuality, Spirituality, Romance and Religion on America's Col-*

lege Campuses. In an interview in *U. S. Catholic* (October 2008), she defines the phenomenon this way: "A hook-up is any sexually intimate activity—it could be as innocent as kissing or it could be intercourse—but what defines it is that it's casual, unplanned, with no commitment. It often involves alcohol and little talking."

The hook-up compulsion flourishes in theme parties—old-time frat house behavior—where the partygoers dress up as pimps and whores. It includes a lot of lying about performance, and it leaves little room for romance or what is classically called "a relationship." Freitas comments about the women caught in this web. "The myth today is that all women love sex and porn....They're actually really unsettled by that attitude. They feel ashamed and uncomfortable." And she adds this, tellingly: "My students didn't know they could have boundaries other than sexual assault and rape."

Mike Hayes, author of *Googling God: The Religious Landscape of People in their 20s and 30s,* has this reflection: "Many young adults stop their spiritual searching with the experience of sensuality....Sensual experiences they find in drug abuse or sexuality is a cheap substitute for what is missing in a deep faith life" (19). Addiction to such pleasures certainly blocks the way to commitment. It affords no firmness of direction; what pleases or satisfies today may be displaced tomorrow. It precludes any kind of readiness to sacrifice, any deferred gratification. And it clouds any larger vision or spiritual dimension, anything threatening to self will and addiction.

A Look at Narcissus

Another tremendous block to commitment is narcissism, the condition of self-absorption. The very name for this navel gazing is witness to its long history. In Greek myth, the handsome youth Narcissus falls in love with his own image reflected in the water and drowns in his passionate attraction to it.

The classical Greeks were anything but self-effacing. Narcissism can infect a person at any age. Children have to be weaned away from it. This intent focus on the self is a special threat to celebrities, with the media and audiences or publics glued to their every move. It has always been so. The renowned tenor, Enrico Caruso, who was in San Francisco on the day of the great earthquake and fire in 1906 with baggage loads of clothing and costumes, seems to have taken the earthquake as a personal affront, as if to say to the earthquake, "How dare you? I am Caruso!" The petulance of opera stars is legendary; but even with the common garden variety of narcissist, nobody needs to be told how to detect them. Only notice the unremitting use of the first-person pronoun.

The phrase "spoiled children" does well as a stand-in for "narcissists." The spoilage is like fruit starting to go bad before it even ripens. The Mexicans have a great word for young people in this condition: *consentidos*. *Niños consentidos* are youngsters whose parents pretty much let them do whatever they want and have whatever they ask for. They are "consented to," whatever the occasion. The single-child family, in particular, risks this phenomenon. The child has no sibling for a reality check, and the parents are prone to keep the spotlight on him or her.

Joan Acocella of *The New Yorker* has reviewed a set of books that use a newer word, "overparenting," to discuss the spoiling of children. In better-off families, she says, there is often a curious combination of hands off and hands on—hands off any restraints to behavior and hands on to whatever will make Johnny or Jane *summa cum laude* one day. Her recipe for prevention is to shut up the kid who is trying to get all the attention at his parents' house party and to let the kid have some playing time on his own that is not part of "a strenuous program of extracurricular activities." She discusses the commercial service IvyWise that is available at a stiff price all through high school, right up to and through college application. The over-anxious parent, the hovering mentor, will maximize the teenager's achievement instead of allowing for a work experience or a service experience which more befits the human growth process.

If you enter into business with a narcissist, to say nothing of entering into a marriage, you are in for a rough ride. Honesty, faithfulness may be forthcoming on the level of conduct, as long as it is productive or satisfying. But in the face of a greater attraction, or when self-sacrifice is called for, or in a crisis, the self-admirer will quickly be out the door. "Stability" is not an operative word for the narcissist. To the extent that narcissism or preoccupation with one's image and one's career and one's curriculum vitae and one's abs and one's amps is rampant, not much commitment can really be looked for.

What Immaturity Feels Like

A much more general condition than hedonism or narcissism is simple immaturity. Call it lesser narcissism, if you wish, because it can eventually be outgrown. The person in question is undeveloped, shallow, and non-battle-tested. He or she sees a lot of options out on the table and has no criterion of choice. One of the options looks good, and he or she chooses it. But then the other one comes up, looking even better; end of allegiance to the first. One signs up for something and then bows out. A person says "yes" to a lot of things—the movie, *Yes Man*, plays on that—but the "yes" does not stick. We are not talking about the person with a strong "P" on the Meyers Briggs personality chart—the person who is over-perceptive, over-pondering when it comes to a series of choices, though that is a problem, too (I can tell you about it). We are talking about the person who jumps too soon, without much awareness or consideration.

Psychologist Scott Peck, in his classic, *The Road Less Traveled*, speaks about immaturity in love—or more directly, the big default in love. By his definition, love is serious business, "the will to extend oneself for the purpose of nurturing one's own or another's spiritual growth." He emphasizes the substantial effort to be made: "When we love someone our love becomes evident or real only through our exertion—through the fact that for someone (or for ourself) we take an extra step or walk an extra mile." This is not romantic love as celebrated in so much popular music.

> Of all the misconceptions about love, the most powerful and widespread is the belief that "falling in love" is love, because we experience it in such a powerful way. It sure feels like it is love. But falling in love is not an act of the will, not a conscious choice. It is specifically a sex-linked erotic experience....
>
> The sudden release of oneself from oneself, the explosive pouring out of oneself into the beloved...is experienced by most people as ecstatic....But the feeling of ecstatic loving-ness always passes, the honeymoon ends....That is when the task of real love begins—to act lovingly when we do not feel that way at all.

Scott Peck wants to indicate the path from immaturity to maturity. Doing so, he provides the linkage to what Marcel Lieberman identifies as the major benefit of commitment, its way of enriching our self-identity.

> The temporary loss of ego boundaries involved in falling in love and in sexual intercourse...leads us to make commitments to other people from which real love may begin.... For a person who grows in real love, over many years of extending himself or herself, there is a gradual and progres-

sive enlargement of the self and identification with much of the world. The feeling of bliss or ecstasy, less dramatic and more gentle, is also more stable and lasting.

Immaturity is not to be taken lightly, though it is a stage we all have to pass through. Often enough, in the marriage tribunal of Catholic dioceses where annulment petitions are considered, the issue is serious immaturity on the part of one spouse or both at the time of marriage. Gathering evidence to substantiate this is a crucial part of making the case before the weighing of evidence. The major question will always be: Was the person in question capable of a commitment—of not just saying but really meaning the words of the marriage vows—at the time? We can ask, of course, whether anybody at age eighteen or twenty or twenty-two, with limited self-experience and no view of the future, is really capable of such a pledge of himself or herself for better or for worse and for life. The remarkable thing is that, yes, it happens frequently. It is part of the miracle of human faith and hopefulness.

A Bow to Maturity

Tobias Wolff, in his recent short story, "Awake" (*The New Yorker;* August 25, 2008), has a contrasting study of maturity and immaturity in two Columbia University students, Ana and Richard. Ana is Russian and not really "his type," as Richard sees it. Somehow, though, he happens to make overtures to her (Wolff makes it sound exactly that random), to which she responds. As the story goes on, they are in bed together, Ana asleep and Richard musing.

They were just having fun, that was how he'd seen it, the two of them having some fun before going their separate ways, as people did, people their age with their whole lives still ahead of them. They didn't want to get tied down now, when they didn't know who they might still meet and what might open up, what chances and adventures.

But Richard one day realized "that Ana had gone all serious on him." What to do now? He knew "it would be wrong to take advantage of her...but then he found that he couldn't break it off, because even with friends, even talking to other girls, he missed her." Goodbye to willpower, Richard. Lying next to her in bed now, as she sleeps, Richard realizes that "Ana was already who she was going to be, and he was not."

His ways of thinking were smaller than hers. He wasn't curious, as she was, didn't like and trust others, as she did, for all the hardships of her life. He complained a lot, and she never complained.

Ana was a noblewoman. O.K., that sounded like something from a book, but it was true. It was just that she'd come to him too soon....She was the one he should have met later, after he'd stuck his neck out and suffered some losses, after he'd really messed things up...and got lost, and kept going anyway—when this little green soul of his had taken some lumps and some weather and bulked up into a man's soul, so that he could look out of his own eyes and not feel like a kid in a mask.

Is there any better way of characterizing maturity and immaturity? One would think not. "Green soul"—how fine a phrase for immaturity.

News From the Quick Message Culture

Mike Hayes, an experienced youth minister in the Chicago area, is one of those who finds distinctive traits in the two most recent generations and probes the effect they may have on religious commitment. (Tom Beaudoin was perhaps the earliest of such analysts in Catholic circles and influential on the thinking of Hayes.) The two cohorts in question are Generation X, those born between 1964 and 1979, including Hayes himself, and their successors, the Millennials, born from 1980 onwards. Hayes has become very familiar with both groups, above all through the Web site he initiated, BustedHalo.com. He has published his findings and conclusions in *Googling God: The Religious Landscape of People in their 20s and 30s.*

Hayes based his title, *Googling God,* on the fact that all of these young adults now expect instant access to information, to music, to friends, the way Google delivers immediate answers and links. They have an innate desire to get meaningful experience quickly. College teachers, however, experience the down side of this impulse in undeveloped habits of reflection and lessened patience with thinking through a proposition. So much is feeding in all the time in a quick-message culture. Slowing down whatever they are consuming, literally or figuratively, seems a big challenge. How, one may ask, can they achieve the self-understanding, "the frameworks of meaning," that Charles Taylor and Marcel Lieberman tell us are essential to make sense of their lives, to say nothing of making a substantive commitment?

Both of these generations, according to Hayes, live "in a world full of noise and images constantly vying for young adults' attention," where contemplative space is at a premium. Yet they differ in major ways. The world was relatively tranquil from the late 70s onwards, when Generation Xers were in their teens and twenties. Their particular atmosphere of thought, conveyed to them in schools and elsewhere, was critical of received thinking and oriented strongly to serving the needy. Even today, Gen Xers do not much feel "an intellectual need for certitude....The majority of the more experienced Generation Xers tend to view the world in a more pluralistic and explorative manner." Due to their skepticism about what is handed down, "experience is at the crux of Generation X's meaning-making mechanism." They do not take root easily in communities of faith. "Generation Xers especially note that they do not often have a solid religious or spiritual home that they can call their own, and this sense of wandering often lends itself to short-term commitments instead of affiliation."

Millennials, especially the younger ones, came of age just as 9/11 rocked the country. They "feel the terror of uncertainty in a world filled with unconscionable and irrational violence....They have grown up as the most watched-over generation in history," which has acted as a brake on their social instincts, their sense of community. The uncertainties of their time have left many of them "longing for certainty and for a God who orders everything and makes sense of their world." Millennial young adults, we are told, "don't possess the critical tools needed for decision making." The more religious among them instead tend to rely on "the guidance of rules, regulations, and personal guides." Mentors are vital to them.

Many Catholic Millennials, impacted by Pope John Paul II, have insisted on connecting to whatever they can of the tradition—capital "T"—both in teaching and worship. "Evangelical young adults have already changed the face of the church in pointing out a need for communities to espouse both the vertical and the horizontal approaches to Catholic tradition."

The Evangelical churches have exercised quite a strong pull on young Millennials. But Evangelical young adults, says Hayes, "have a tough time navigating moments of ambiguity, especially death and vocational change." And guess what? "Young adults will likely change careers, not merely jobs, three times in their lifetime." They will have major change to cope with frequently.

Such are the profiles of the two most recent generations of young American adults, as proposed today by an astute observer, by no means alone, from their own number. Generalities of this sort can be easily belied, but they have value here as indicating weaknesses that can block commitment in one of its three essential features: stability, orientation to action, and accrued self-understanding. The profiles also indicate the strengths, the resources they have to draw on.

What about those of us no longer Millennial or Generation X, perhaps even far from it? We all live in this hurried, instant-access world, with the cell phone in our pocket and purse and text messaging underway all around us. In our centrifuge of individualism, we much welcome the call to community. And we all need frequent renewal of our courage and clearing of a vision in parlous times.

"What Must I do?"

Karl Rahner, the pioneering theologian of the last mid-century, spoke of young people, in his day, as "infinite questioners." It is still true that they can go for hours in their own groups hashing over all the serious topics. (These used to be called "bull sessions.") In the communities of faith, as in society otherwise, young adults are resistant to marshalling and requirements, says Hayes. He adds, "the more we require of people today, the less commitment we will get in return." What the young do respond to, he adds, in capital letters, is Direct Personal Initiative. Before a marriage under Catholic auspices today, the couple is bound to a six-month period of preparation. There are some essential steps to this process, but they matter only if they engage the real concerns and questions of the marrying parties.

Suppose we consider the young adult in the Gospels who comes up to Jesus, asking, "What must I do to inherit eternal life?" (Mark 10:17–22). He has been observant, in terms of the Torah. Conscious of the Ten Commandments, God's behavioral guides, he has kept them well. Yet he recognizes something lacking. The response of Jesus is to challenge him: "Jesus, looking at him, loved him and said to him, 'You are lacking one thing. Go, sell what you have, and give to the poor and you will have treasure in heaven; then come, follow me'" (Mark 10:21). Jesus spoke literally; his calling was to be on the road.

These words awaken the young adult to the restraints upon him. He has a lot that he is attached to—great audio equipment, a pilot's license, a health club membership, a couple of master's degrees. Let loose of it all?! "At that statement his face fell, and he went away sad, for he had many possessions" (Mark 10:22) The generosity that leads young people into tutoring or into years of volunteer service or to strongly espousing a cause, in short, to leaving a lot of "stuff" behind them, that is what a commitment—at any age—calls for.

4

A Cloud Over Commitment

Climate Changes in the Church

I n the 1950s and 1960s, Father Pierre Teilhard de Chardin, SJ, fired up the Catholic world and much of the intellectual world with his book, *The Phenomenon of Man*. It described the whole planet as involved in a process not just of growing complexity but of unification, with divine energies at work to create a unified environment of spirit that he called the Noosphere. This great paleontologist and seer accurately observed the Global Village in process, and it made him tremendously hopeful. He could not have known in the 1950s the pitched battles and gross unfairness and widespread affliction that would go on in this big town.

A Dominican priest, Father Raymond Nogar, was almost the sole cautionary voice in his book, *The Lord of the Absurd*. Basing himself on the story and the theology of the passion and cross of Christ, Father Nogar issued a series of caveats about Teilhard. A reviewer, D. A. Drennen, summed it up in *America* Magazine (September 3, 1966): "Fr. Nogar sets himself both scientifically and religiously against the cosmic optimism and convergence-theology of Teilhard de Chardin." De Chardin, he says, "represents the orderliness of nature...where chaos is always submerged in concord and logic continually conquers contradiction." Nogar was claiming, on the contrary, that the God of the late twentieth century is more fittingly the God of evolutionary chance, historic risk, calamity, and desperation."

The writings of Father Teilhard emerged into the light just as the Church came marching enthusiastically out of the Second Vatican Council in the mid-sixties. That was the Council that struck such an encouraging motif at the start of its closing document, *The Pastoral Constitution Gaudium et Spes* ("The Church in the Modern World"): "The joy and hope, the grief and anguish of the men of our time, especially of those who are poor or afflicted in any way, are the joy and hope, the grief and anguish of the followers of Christ as well." This is still an inspiring message!

The theologian Karl Rahner, who had been a major force in the Vatican Council, admitted towards the end of his life that the Council had underestimated the obstacles. "We represented and lived an optimism that has been only partially fulfilled in the developments of the last decades," he said. "The Council's decree, *Gaudium et Spes*, can be blamed, despite all that is right in it, for underestimating sin, the social consequences of human guilt, the horrible possibilities of running into historical dead ends, and so on." (Interview with László Zeley, *Faith in a Wintry Season*.)

Father Rahner went on to comment that if theologians still hope for universal salvation, "it is because this optimism belongs precisely to the absurdity of the cross, to which we are bound as messengers of hope in God over against the hopelessness of humankind." The revelations of sexual abuse and inaction by Church superiors was to come very shortly. The Catholic landscape darkened considerably.

The feeling of discouragement is caught live by the fine Irish writer, William Trevor, in his short story, "Justina's Priest" (*A Bit on the Side*). Young Justina, mentally weak, has attached herself to Father Clohessy, the local pastor, who takes a crucial step to shield her from harm, and he succeeds at it. The dutiful man, however, has a cloud over him, a "general feeling of deprivation that, these days, he was not often without." And Trevor explains why.

> The grandeur of his Church had gone, leaving his priesthood within it bleak, the vocation that had beckoned him less insistent than it had been. He had seen his congregations fall off and struggled against the feeling that he had been deserted. Confusion spread from the mores of the times into the Church itself; in combating it, he prayed for guidance but was not heard.

Karl Rahner once more had the right word for what is going on in Father Clohessy's Ireland and elsewhere. He points out that with the widening of human possibilities, the options people have, "the Christian in this historical situation at once discovers the sharply painful nature of choice." He finds this smorgasbord of choices today to be "carrying with it both the pain and the noble potentialities of freedom," overwhelmingly. Rahner made this point in his lecture, "The Present Situation of Christians: A Theological Interpretation of the Position of Christians in the Modern World." He published it in *The Christian Commitment*, Sheed and Ward, 1963. As the title of his book indicates, the big choice, in Rahner's mind, comes down to the question, "What values, what set of priorities, what conception of human purpose, what much larger picture or, to sum it up, what commitment will characterize my life?"

Note that Rahner, speaking in 1963, locates his topic specifically in "this present age, the end-product of the modern period." What he said was in the vein of the great German preacher and spiritual writer, Romano Guardini, and Guardini's apocalyptic book, *The End of Modern Times (Die Ende der Neuzeit)*. A strong sense of closure apparently was coming to this era of breakthrough achievement that, as a cultural phenomenon, we have entitled "modernism."

Post-Modernism: Is Life a Joke?

The change of climate in the Church, from euphoria to what Rahner called, in his 1989 interview, an "optimism [that] belongs precisely to the absurdity of the cross," did not come without its counterpart in the world at large. In those heady days of the 1960s and early 1970s, days of the Beatles and Woodstock, which were also, alas, the time of the Vietnam War and calamitous assassinations, the climate of the world was headed into a red shift, a whole modified set of perceptions and attitudes to be known eventually as postmodern. That is the air that people breathe today in a sadder but wiser epoch that has called into question the very possibility of commitment. Anthony Campbell, an Australian Jesuit, put this well in his book, *God First Loved Us, 2000*: "Agnostics believe they cannot know enough to commit themselves."

The noxious impact can be measured in a recent experience of a friend of mine on the streets of Hollywood. Out walking one afternoon, he suddenly took ill and was obviously in some distress. A young man, noticing this, came up to him and offered some polite and practical help. After the urgency had subsided somewhat, my friend thanked him warmly. The young man, for his part, shrugged and replied, "Take care of yourself; life is a joke."

Life as a cruel joke: is that the message of postmodernism? Judging from dramas being written and staged widely, one is tempted to think so. The young man above fits right into a description of "the wounded postmodernist," by Joseph Feeney, SJ, in a vignette he derived from conversation with his university students: "His emotions are exhausted, his expectations minimal, his hopes few. And he protects himself with humor." As one of Feeney's students told him, "I make fun of everything and poke at the status quo" ("Can a Worldview Be Healed? Students and Postmodernism," *America* Magazine; November 15, 1997).

William Shakespeare, who was so prescient, shows us Hamlet

in a similar, world-weary frame of mind. Having just returned from the university, Hamlet appreciates the Renaissance take on the greatness of man—"What a piece of work is a man! How noble in reason!" (*Hamlet*, Act II, Scene ii). Nevertheless the ghostly revelation that his father the king was murdered by his uncle, who also seduced the queen, has left him "sicklied over by the pale cast of thought" (Act III). It has reduced to ashes this image of human greatness. "And yet, to me, what is this quintessence of dust?" (Act II). He can focus only on fragility and mortality.

Shakespeare catches the acedia, the sapping of energy and emotion, which has afflicted his princely hero. In its classic definition, acedia is "the lack of commitment to spiritual values, or carelessness, listlessness, unconcern." The person "experiences a great deal of unhappiness and disappointment in life, though sometimes this is cloaked by cynicism" (*The New Dictionary of Catholic Spirituality*, 4). Hamlet says to his foils, Rosencrantz and Guildenstern, "I have of late—but wherefore I know not—lost all my mirth, forgone all custom of exercises, and indeed it goes so heavily with my disposition that this goodly frame the earth seems to me a sterile promontory."

Postmodernism as a mindset does not have to land one at such extremes, but it can still deeply affect all of one's outlook. Its more normal form is a cool attitude. One is determined never to be shocked. One is ever skeptical about institutions and received truths. As for the artists, they resist having to resolve discord. "[They] reduce what they consider rational communication (verbalizations, precise visual references) and pursue new subjective forms to express primary emotions (force, eroticism, fright) smothered by dominant conventions" (*Hybrid Cultures*, Néstor García Canclini; translated by Christopher Chiappari and Silvia Lopez). Harold Pinter, among modern dramatists, set this mode.

Signs of the Times According to Cardinal Martini

Cardinal Carlo Martini, the retired archbishop of Milan, has spelled out the challenges of postmodernism today in "Teaching the Faith in a Postmodern World" (*America* Magazine; May 12, 2008). "Nowadays," he says, "there is a little of everything on the same plain, because there are no longer criteria by which to verify what is a true and authentic civilization." Rationality is suspect, is out, because it is seen as doing violence to people, especially in authoritarian systems which impose their way. "There is acceptance of every form of dialogue and exchange because of a desire to be always open to one another and to what is different." Openness, tolerance, has become a shibboleth…The postmodern mind has taken to itself the "Uncertainty Principle" of the great physicist Werner Heisenberg, who found that, in stellar calculation, the observer's standpoint—the active presence of a subject, colors—to some extent warps all the data. This principle about a necessary bias that needs to be figured into observation is not a flat-out statement that everything is relative. Many have taken it so, however, claiming it allows a plurality of "truths"—your truth is yours, and mine is mine.

At best, truth is much more tentative for a lot of younger people. So what does one rely on for norms? One relies on agreement, shared outlook within one's particular community or coterie and, above all, on personal experience. The accent on experience is, as Mike Hayes observed in *Googling God*, primary for young adults today.

Cardinal Martini sketches out the dire effect that postmodern thinking has on religious outlook: "There is no more sin, nor pardon, nor redemption, nor self-denial. Life can no longer be thought of as sacrifice or suffering." Still, remarkably enough, in this era when "diversity" has become such a slogan, he finds an opening for a healthy response.

Perhaps this situation is better than the one that existed previously. Christianity has an opportunity to show better its character of challenge, of objectivity, of realism, of the exercise of true freedom, of a religion linked to the life of the body and not only of the mind. In a world such as we live in today, the mystery of an unavailable and always surprising God acquires greater beauty; faith understood as risk becomes more attractive; a tragic view of existence is strengthened with happy consequences in contrast to a purely evolutionary vision.

These words make me reflect on a fellow Jesuit of my own generation whom I have long been considering postmodern. I have found myself taken aback sometimes at his starting point of doubt and suspicion in dealing with statements presented as authoritative or binding. His Christian belief nonetheless is solidly grounded. It is just that after decades of challenging and helping university students, both American and Asian, to clarify what their own values are, he recoils from the role of sure interpreter. When pushed, however, he has not hesitated to say what he holds to firmly, which strikes me as the essential.

A Swim Against the Tide

Observing how the cultural and intellectual climate militates against putting one's chips on any long-term bet, a person could wonder if any commitment at all is safe to make. The first thing to do in response is to cross out the word "safe." To challenge odds, to swim against the tide, is risk-taking behavior, for which one must be courageous. Safety cannot be the consideration so much as the awareness that I cannot but do such and such. Consider some situations:

- I have just been at the Wharton School and am primed for the business world, yet the Peace Corps draws me strongly. I cannot but respond.
- I have really sweated to build up my savings. If I sink them into starting this little business, I could lose it all fast. Yet this is what I have always looked forward to doing. I cannot but.
- This big student loan I need could be a ball and chain on me for years, and all my family discourages it, but I want to be a vet, period. And the med school has accepted me. I cannot but.
- This sweetheart of mine is not the dream man or the best I can do. I know him too well. But we share so much, and our hearts are set on one another. It is in the cards.

I remember my own awareness, as my ordination date was approaching, that all other doors were closing. How full of drawbacks I was for the demands ahead. Which way to go? I focused on a passage in John's Gospel, where Jesus had just announced, "Unless you eat the flesh of the Son of Man and drink his blood, you do not have life within you" (6:53). His disciples found this a hard saying, and we are told that many turned away. Jesus then said to the Twelve, "Do you also want to turn away?" Simon Peter spoke for the rest, "Master, to whom shall we go? You have the words of eternal life." That was what I needed to hear.

In Favor of Magnanimity

The good of the world, after all, depends on moral courage. Aristotle, the sage who has left such an imprint upon European philosophy, was not unaware of this. In the moral guidelines he left us, a treatise we now know as *The Nichomachean Ethics*, he singled out magnanimity as the peak, the quality most vital for the good of society and for galvanizing human potential. What does "magnanimity" connote to us? Greatness of soul, generosity and daring.

Saint Ignatius Loyola, after his dramatic and costly initiation to the spiritual life, developed a set of Spiritual Exercises for those wishing guidance on the same pathway. He points out that all who undertake the Exercises "will benefit greatly by entering upon them with great spirit and generosity toward their Creator and Lord and by offering all their desires and freedom to him." Ignatius had the charism of the saints, greatness of soul.

How much I admire those medical pioneers in our times, Doctors without Borders (*Médecins sans Frontieres*), who go into the thick of turmoil and violence to care for the injured and infected. If that be not magnanimity and commitment, what is? In his novel, *The Plague*, Albert Camus celebrated just such a fictional hero, Doctor Rieux, fighting the bubonic scourge in Oran, Algeria. Camus and hence Doctor Rieux were both existentialist, dubious about any meaning or religious dimension to life. But somehow or other, that fed their moral courage, their commitment.

Magnanimity, generosity, this is what Cardinal Martini has in mind, I am convinced, urging us to keep the faith, to stand up for something substantive in an unpromising milieu. In the First Letter of John, we get the gist of what Martini is driving at. "I write to you, young men, because you are strong and the word of God remains in you, and you have conquered the evil one. Do not love the world or the things of the world...." (1 John 2:14–15). This stricture against love of the world may sound like the opposite of Doctor Rieux and Doctors Without Borders. It is not. The "world," or the worldliness, that the Letter of John warns about is identified as "sensual lust, enticement for the eyes, and a pretentious life" (1 John 2:16). This manner of indulgence undermines all great human enterprises.

Our reflections on the postmodern challenge may well conclude with the last book of the New Testament, the Apocalypse or Revelation. This is not an easy Scripture to read or digest, because there is so much in its visions or imaginings that seems counter to our sense of the merciful Savior. Dread cosmic chastisements descend upon the many sinners of the planet, wiping them out two or three times over. But we do get the point of God being definitely done with "the world," that is, with all forces of selfishness and self-indulgence resistant to the message of Jesus Christ.

The purpose of the vivid presentations of the Apocalypse is to bolster those choosing to live out their hard-bought faith in the teeth of Roman paganism, which could be so dismissive and cruel. The Apocalypse, however wildly and even vindictively it may have been interpreted over the ages, was written for new followers of the Way, to confirm their Christian commitment. That makes it very contemporary.

5

"How Should I Presume?"

One of my favorite poems over the years has been the pioneer poem of the modernist era, "The Love Song of J. Alfred Prufrock," by T. S. Eliot. Not only is it innovative and brilliant as a poem; it also, I have always felt, is about me. It is full of the self-doubts of a very correct young man, whose very name declares him to be of a proper, buttoned-up family. We can see him as he describes himself: "My morning coat, my collar mounting firmly to the chin, / My necktie rich and modest, but asserted by a simple pin." That pin is about as much assertion as Prufrock can manage.

The "love song" in the title is ironic. Prufrock would "love" to approach one of the female sophisticates at a party in good society, but has to ask himself dubiously, " 'Do I dare?' and 'Do I dare?' " He is skittish about making any romantic move, imagining that the airy young women will make fun of him. And he is all too aware of still having time to exit. "Do I dare?" is a motif of the poem, and it reappears at a humorous extreme towards the very end, "Do I dare to eat a peach?" The motif also occurs in another wording that has long stuck in my memory. The hapless young man, thinking of the females he would dearly love to approach, has to keep chiding himself: "And how should I presume?"

To sum it up, J. Alfred Prufrock finds himself bound up pretzel tight, all initiative stymied. These were the 1910s, when Freud was writing and lecturing on inhibition, and T. S. Eliot had found its perfect imaginative form. As a Harvard undergrad from a family with some link to Bostonian society, he was drawing on the environment he knew.

Eliot's Prufrock is not shallow. He is aware of the big existential questions and of models of heroism and of the social problems in the city about him, but he is intimidated from uttering these concerns. He can envision his moment of greatness, but at the same time he imagines a snicker from the wings and admits to the hearer of his 'song': "And in short, I was afraid." To say that this invented person is a long way from commitment would be to hammer on the obvious. Prufrock cannot even take a first timid step. But his repeated question, "And how should I presume?" is very much amplified in the postmodern era.

The Buried Talent

Prufrock look alikes have been on earth for a long time. The Bible lets us know this. There is nothing really of consequence in human experience that does not come under inspection somewhere in the Bible. Consider, for example, the parable of the talents, Matthew 25:14–30. "It will be as when a man who was going on a journey called in his servants and entrusted his possessions to them. To one he gave five talents; to another, two; to a third, one—to each according to his ability. Then he went away."

A talent, we are informed, was "a unit of coinage of high but varying value depending on its metal (gold, silver, copper) and its place of origin" (the *New American Bible*, footnote to Matthew 18:24). The one who received five talents went right to work trading with it and made another five. The man receiving two did likewise, doubling his two. Whether by banking, trading, or commerce, each of these men risked losing their principal. Who doesn't know that the market is always risky? So the man who received one talent, to preserve it, "went off and dug a hole in the ground and buried his master's money."

When the master came back, the man who had squirreled away his one talent had to come forward and explain himself. He said, "Master, I knew you were a demanding person, harvesting where you did not plant and gathering where you did not scatter; so out of fear I went off and buried your talent in the ground. Here it is back." The master is furious. He not only strips the talent from "this useless servant," he casts him into the outer darkness, "where there will be wailing and grinding of teeth."

In this parable, Jesus did not intend to teach that God is a severe and harsh master—far from it. The cautious man, however, had let this idea get into his head and paralyze him. Jesus wanted to teach that each of us is particularly gifted and thereby called to make the most of what we are and have, in God's service. He wanted to insist: Let not fearfulness have its way. It helps to notice that the parable of the talents appears in the chapter of Matthew's Gospel concentrating on the final judgment. There are both wise and foolish attitudes in view of our eventual judgment. To be a "good and faithful servant," initiative is called for; commitment is expected. The wailing and grinding of teeth results from getting it all wrong.

The Catechism of the Catholic Church tells us that, through the mediation of the Church, each individual receives 'talents' that enrich his or her identity and that the person must render them fruitful, for the good of the community (see CCC 1880). Admittedly our talents differ according to age, physical capacities, intellectual or moral aptitude, resources, and favorable circumstances, the Catechism says. Distribution is not equal, but that opens the opportunity for each to share what he or she has received, and to look to others for their strong example and liberality (CCC 1936–37).

A People Good at Fearing

n our own day and age, the age of entrepreneurship, we need to meditate on the parable of the talents. The question, repeated twice by Eliot, " 'Do I dare?' and 'Do I dare?' " resonates today. I would not have started this book if I did not think so. A generation later than Prufrock, during the Depression of the 1930s, an American president, Franklin Delano Roosevelt, had to harangue the country in these terms: "The only thing we have to fear is fear itself, nameless, unreasoning, unjustified terror, which paralyzes needed efforts to convert retreat into advance." Roosevelt sensed the crying need of confidence—in banks, in markets, in American resilience—to get the country back on its feet. That was a hard sell to the men and women in the bread lines, but it was crucial that they somehow be buoyed.

Today, as bailouts by the billions seek to restore our confidence that the economy is sound, and as experts look anxiously at unemployment figures, those same jitters are paramount. This was the recent assessment by Julie Hanus in her article "Fear Itself" in (*Utne* Magazine). She mentions that sociologists have a term, "risk society," for "cultures increasingly preoccupied with threats to safety, both real and perceived." In our country, the threats, to her mind, are more perceived than real.

That is a view echoed by Jan Hoffman in her article for the *New York Times* entitled, "Why Can't She Walk to School?" (September 12, 2009). Fear of child abduction keeps parents from letting their young walk even a few blocks to school. The possibilities of such an event are minimal, Hoffman contends, not worth stifling a normal stage of growing up.

Elements of security that we take for granted today hardly existed a couple of generations ago—gated communities, video surveillance, permits for concealed weapons. The most noxious of these elements are car alarms, because they go off at any disturbance, and no one is ever around to shut them off. Consider the great "Information Highway," so incredibly advantageous. It is also perceived as a bandit-infested road that one dare not travel without virus protection. And consider issues in the public forum—immigration, healthcare reform, alternates to incarceration. Fear in the air has people yelling and politicians or radio punsters playing on them shamelessly.

Fear creeps or seeps. It imbues and colors things. Umperceptibly, it can narrow our viewpoint and restrict our choices. Fear has to be playing some hidden or not so hidden role these days in the preponderance of couples living together without marriage. The phenomenon has other causes, to be sure, economic and cultural. But how about fear also, as an element that cannot be discounted—fear of commitment, nothing more or less? It is fed by the following worries: Who can trust anything or anyone long-term any more? How can we take on the expense and demands of children, given our tenuous careers? How can we presume to take oaths or formal vows? The remarkable thing is that so many young people still take the leap, with formal blessings and much family support, sanguine about their futures.

"Papa, Aren't You Afraid?"

The great enemy, humanly speaking, is death, especially if it is viewed as one's eclipse, one's extinction, with nothing more beyond. If we look around at the animal kingdom, from insects on up, we see a remarkable and fierce resistance when the end is threatened. How much do we allow fear of death to affect us?

A Turkish poet, Nazin Hikmet, talks of the courage necessary for living:

There is no shame in dreading death
Or thoughts of dying.

The strangest of our powers
Is the courage to live
Knowing that we will die,
Knowing nothing more true.

TRANSLATED BY RANDY BLASING AND MUTLU KONUK
AMERICAN POETRY REVIEW, MAY/JUNE 2001

Hikmet's assertion of "no shame" is comforting to me, who has long wrestled with this enemy, fear of death, in my unguarded thoughts. Nonetheless, I admire William Faulkner's assertion, in his Nobel Prize speech: "The basest of all things is to be afraid." Blessed are people like Juan Salvador, the father and central figure in Victor Villaseñor's novel, *Rain of Gold*, based largely on his own father and family of birth. In his last illness, one of his children asks him, "Papa, aren't you afraid?" He answers, "Of what? Of death? To fear death is to insult life." To fear death is also to insult one's faith.

The New Testament letter known as Hebrews reminds its Jewish Christian readers that death, when undergone by Jesus, gave up its power. He freed "those who through fear of death had been subject to slavery all their life" (2:15). Confidence in God's care, even in the face of death, is the very touchstone of the religious spirit. That was the opinion of the psychologist Erik Erikson, although he agreed that religion often has the exact opposite effect. "Trust born of care," he wrote in *Childhood and Society*, "is the touchstone of the actuality of a given religion. All religions have in common the periodical childlike surrender to a Provider or providers who dispense earthly fortune as well as spiritual health."

"Shouldn't the Second Coming of Christ be a fearful consideration?" Saint Augustine once asked his congregation. "Quite the opposite," he answered.

"HOW SHOULD I PRESUME?" ◀ 59

He who is without anxiety waits without fear until his Lord comes. For what sort of love of Christ is it to fear his coming? Brothers, do we not have to blush for shame? We love him, yet we fear his coming. Are we really certain that we love him?

SERMON ON PSALM 95

Is it Wise to Fear the Lord?

A very big problem can arise for any diligent Christian, any Bible reader, despite this stirring outburst from Saint Augustine. It is the phrase "fear of the Lord" which, although we do not really hear it in the New Testament, permeates the Wisdom writings of the Old Testament and is heard in half of the Psalms. The fullest statement of this spiritual concept appears at the start of the book called The Wisdom of Sirach, 1:9–12.

> Fear of the Lord is glory and splendor,
>   gladness and a festive crown.
> Fear of the Lord warms the heart,
>   giving gladness and joy and length of days.
> He who fears the Lord will have a happy end;
>   even on the day of his death he will be blessed.
> The beginning of wisdom is fear of the Lord,
>   which is formed with the faithful in the womb.

I spent recent years in the presence of a spiritual director of priests who was so allergic to that biblical phrase "fear of the Lord" that he could not stand to hear it. He was all too aware of the long history of the Church trying to convert sinners by imagery of God's anger, rather than a stress on God's kindness or forgiveness. He took as his mantra The First Letter of John: "Perfect love drives out fear" (4:18). The whole sentence reads: "There is no fear in love, but perfect love drives out fear because fear has to do with punishment, and so one who fears is not yet perfect in love." The above spiritual director argued for every instance of "fear the Lord" in the Bible to be transmuted into "revere the Lord," because that is the positive charge that the biblical sources want to communicate. But that is not about to happen.

What we do need to do is connect fear/revere and love/serve the way the Book of Deuteronomy, at the heart of the Torah, intended: "What does the Lord, your God, ask of you but to fear the Lord, your God, and follow his ways exactly, to love and serve the Lord, your God, with all your heart and all your soul, to keep the commandments and statutes of the Lord which I enjoin on you today for your own good?" (10:12–13). Note that, above, fear is put in tandem with love, and that the Scripture brings together faith and loving conduct.

In the Latin-American edition of *Nueva Biblia Española*, the translators, Luis Alonso Schokel, SJ, and Juan Mateos, SJ, commenting on *temor de Dios*, or fear of the Lord, point out that "in its original sense fear of God is…awe of the creature in the presence of God; it is increased by the consciousness of sin." They go on to say, "With time, the concept 'fear' comes to designate the religious feeling and, in terms of the Covenant, faithfulness." Another way to say "faithfulness" is, of course, "keeping to one's commitment."

"Fear Not, O Worm Jacob"

The Bible is the story of weak and fallible humanity being enabled little by little to respond to the divine spouse. The fragile heroes of sacred history, starting with Abraham, need bolstering all the time from the divine message, "Fear not." "Fear not, O worm Jacob, O maggot Israel," the Lord says through Isaiah the prophet (41:14). Pretty startling! The angel Gabriel had to say this to Mary, at the annunciation. Jesus had to say it to his disciples, as in the storm on the lake. "O you of little faith, why did you fear?" In his brief transfiguration on Mount Tabor, when his three closest disciples see his glory, they fall to the ground terrified. He has to come near and touch them: "Rise, and do not be afraid" (17: 7).

After the Last Supper, in his farewell speech to his disciples, Jesus tries to drive the message home: "Do not let your hearts be troubled or afraid" (John 14:27). Father Raymond Brown, in the *Anchor Bible* commentary on John, reminds us how crucial it was for Jesus to hearten his Apostles, since his "departure involves a combat with the Prince of this world."

"Do not fear," means, in practice, "do not let it get the better of you." The psychologist Scott Peck reminds us that fear and courage are not at all incompatible.

> Courage is not the absence of fear; it is the making of action in spite of fear, the moving out against the resistance engendered by fear into the unknown and into the future. On some level, spiritual growth, and therefore love, always requires courage and involves risk.
>
> THE ROAD LESS TRAVELED

The astounding thing—astounding if we lose sight of the real humanity of Jesus—is that our Savior is himself filled with fear at the prospect of his passion and death. "My soul is troubled now," he admits to his Apostles (John 12:27). A cry is wrung out of him: "My Father, if it is possible, let this cup pass from me" (Matthew 26:39). Of course, the plea is provisional. "It is up to you and not me" he is admitting to the Father when he adds, "yet not as I will, but as you will." The letter known as Hebrews puts it unforgettably: "In the days when he was in the flesh, he offered prayers and supplications with loud cries and tears to the one who was able to save him from death, and he was heard because of his reverence" (5: 7).

The last words of Jesus on the cross, according to the Gospel of John, are "It is finished." In other words, "It is accomplished." We have to hear this as putting a cap on his lifelong commitment. Jesus was saying, in effect, "What we decided I would do and endure, for the salvation of the world, what I have never swerved from embracing and doing, is here brought to completion." Is there any more awesome moment?

From Fear to Boldness

We know that fear overcame the disciples totally during the passion and death of Jesus. Only the holy women and "the beloved disciple" dared to show themselves. But what a different picture these all too wobbly creatures present in The Acts of the Apostles. The Jewish leadership is astonished by their boldness. "Observing the boldness of Peter and John and perceiving them to be uneducated, ordinary men, they were amazed" (4:13). The word "boldness"—*parrhesía*, in Greek—becomes dominant in the era just after the resurrection of Jesus and the Pentecostal outpouring of his Spirit. They had been enabled to take up a commitment with unflagging energy. They could respond without any wavering or trepidation to their calling.

This level of boldness was not only evident at every stage of the Acts of the Apostles, it has been a gift of the Holy Spirit to the Church ever since. We have all been witness to it when people act with moral courage in jeopardy to their own interests, or when the terminally infirm carry their burden lightly. I was privileged to see the extremes of commitment, stimulated by faith, during human rights delegations to El Salvador and Central America in the 1980s. Leaders of a national teachers' union met with us under the most guarded circumstances. In what was a police state, church congregations talked and sang pointedly of Christian freedom. Social activists in prison showed us signs of their torture. Above all, The Mothers of the Disappeared, those humblest of women, stepped out of their native diffidence with mourning and bold demands for accounting.

I remember a priest in Uruguay, during a time of draconian tactics by a military government to crush a revolutionary movement, who had an office of counseling and defense for some of the accused. His own period of jail and torture left a line of cigarette burns visible up and down his arm. Yet he was afterwards without recriminations, extending kindness, for example, to his torturer, whom he later met on the city streets.

I remember with reverence the Jesuits whom I had gotten to know at the Central American University in San Salvador, who paid with their lives for vocally espousing social justice. Most of them were animated Basques, keen on soccer; but as Revelation says of the earliest martyrs under Roman rule, "Love for life did not deter them from death" (12:11). Do we need examples of commitment—*compromiso*? There they are. Go and do likewise, the Gospels say to us.

6

Hope, the Fuel of Commitment

Enough of the Discouragements

The last three chapters have been about the obstacles and road blocks to commitment—immaturity, negativity, a timorous spirit. What a formidable trio—the malformed ego, concentrating on "me"; chronic dissatisfaction, thinking "darkness covers the earth"; existential anxiety, worrying about what to bank on. No wonder so many are daunted!

Has anything been left out of this shadowy picture? Yes, decidedly, the sense of what it means to be human. Enough of the parcel of discouragements. Suppose we begin with imagination, initiative, generosity, joyfulness, courage, and that old-fashioned staple, character. Here is what one of the early Fathers of the Church, the martyr Saint Cyprian, bishop of Carthage, said about character:

> The spirit of a strong and stable character strengthened by meditation endures, this unshaken spirit, which is strengthened by a certain and solid faith in the future will be enlivened against all the terrors of the devil and threats of this world.
>
> *Treatise to Fortunatus*

Bishop Cyprian has certainly here laid the foundations for commitment. This is how we are meant to be when setting a course, taking a leap. To have character, to be able to say no under pressure of inducements. To be steadfast, with our course set firmly, despite all that would shake us. To be reliable in promise keeping, as was Jesus Christ, "For the Son of God…was not 'yes' and 'no,' but 'yes' has been in him" (2 Corinthians 1:19). This is how we are meant to be.

Experience shows over and over how vital it is to have a consuming interest. We are made to be fired up. Paul Coelho put this very well in his allegorical novel, *The Alchemist*: "There is a language in the world that everyone understands…the language of enthusiasm; of things accomplished with love and purpose, and as part of a search for something believed in and desired."

The teen years are where the consuming interest seems to be crucial. I remember with gratitude a high school teacher who, knowing how keen I was on writing, roped me into his project of creating a news magazine in the style of *Time*, which was more self-consciously Homeric then than now. I spent most of my junior and senior year on this activity, doing most of the work, with himself as an excellent mentor. How many scientists, male and female, to say nothing of musicians and professional athletes, have gotten their start this way, spurred to excellence early? How many young people droop on the vine or go the way of gangs, for lack of such an encouragement and challenge?

Instances of Hope

On a daily basis, while we look around our world trying to make sense of it, all too aware of the dark tinge, we must not leave out the signs of hope. A priest with whom I live in community loves to come up with signs of hope—instances of generosity, of courage, of joyfulness, of anything that contradicts the law of entropy and reverses the tendency to find clay feet on all public figures. The signs are most often small, and sometimes it takes an obituary to learn of them.

Bill Moyers, in his television special, "Beyond our Differences," told of a woman who for decades had worked in a hospital basement wrapping the surgical instruments ordered for the next operation. On her retirement, she revealed that every time she had finished and sent off a bundle, she had prayed for the patient. Upon hearing this, another woman doing the same work confessed she did the same. They had given themselves this generous and hidden commitment.

Remember the young man who stepped up with a flower before the tank sent into Tienanmen Square to quell the protesters? That gesture gets repeated more often than we realize. One young man in Utah inserted himself into bidding for oil properties that the government was opening up so as to delay what looked like an environmental giveaway. Even crises such as the genocide in Rwanda yield unforgettable bravery, such as that recorded in the movie, *Hotel Rwanda*. It is told also that girls in a boarding school in Rwanda, a half-and-half ethnic mix, were pressed to reveal who among them were the hated Tutsis. They refused, and all went to death together.

The dog-eat-dog world, even if taken literally, is not always that. In the autumn of 2008, people on the Internet were passing around photos taken above the Arctic Circle, where a polar bear arrived to a place where sled dogs were chained. The owner of the dogs quite expected them to become part of the bear's foodchain. But no, what the bear had in mind was playing with the dogs, hugging and tussling with them. The behemoth came back every evening that week for more of the same. This is the world represented at the opening of Genesis, not hostile at all. It is the peaceable kingdom so often represented in paintings by the Quaker artist Edward Hicks. It is the world that God pronounced good.

Hope Keeps on Pushing Us

Hope indeed is what makes the world go. Hope, that is, the expectation of eventual good deriving from what one does or endures, is what drives people to volunteer service. Hope, not money, impels young men and women through lengthy studies for professions, such as nursing, that aim at the good of others. Hope is what launches reform movements, including even political campaigns. The ambience of hope is what makes the wedding ceremony and the reception afterwards special, despite the folderol and the deafening music. The gaze toward the future says, "I hope in you for us." Why are we so moved and grateful at ordinations or vow ceremonies, if not for the renewed hope for the people of God?

Hope and commitment are so intertwined, so mutually inclusive! Hope is the fuel of commitment. For that reason, it will be well here to distill the ingredients of hope. One has to begin, though, with the admission that something has to be missing for hope to be in play. By definition, hope excludes a clear vision or presence of its object. Its reach is towards the impalpable. For example, when two hopefuls pledge to be true to each other in sickness and in health, for richer and for poorer, something of great worth has to be lying ahead, but it is blocked from view. A great goal, like reversing pollution of the ocean, may absorb someone who is dedicated to it, but the result lies way off in the future.

If we did not know the above already by instinct, we could learn it from Saint Paul: "In hope we were saved. Now hope that sees for itself is not hope. For who hopes for what one sees? But if we hope for what we do not see, we wait with endurance" (Romans 8:24–5). Waiting with endurance may sound like just barely hanging on, and sometimes it comes down to that. But the virtue of hope is a positive impulse. It calls us to be responsive and, at its best, enthusiastic, much to the wonder of those who have little or none of it.

One of the old classics in such matters, *The Spiritual Life*, by Adolphe Tanquerey, 1930, isolates three qualities of hope. First of all, there has to be an effective desire, a real push of the heart, that sidelines everything else. Gerard Manley Hopkins, entering consecrated life in the Jesuit order, accepted that his love for poetry and art would take a backseat to his religious vocation, and it did so for some years, until his Jesuit superior stepped in and urged him back toward actively writing. Secondly, there has to be a confident expectation that the object of desire can be reached. The desire in question should ultimately be for the vision of God, or union with God, but we may translate that, on the mundane level, as a better world, a strong marriage, a fruitful profession. The third element in hope is what Tanquerey calls "a commensurate commitment of one's life." This means we move off dead center towards what we hope; we take the requisite steps, we make the necessary pledge, and enter upon a serious follow through. To put it briefly, we proceed with the commitment.

An Eye Is Opened

t is this third step, the resolute action, that defines us. It brings us the self-understanding that, according to Marcel Lieberman, issues from commitment. T. S. Eliot, during his search for meaning in the dark times after World War I, while groping at the same time toward maturity of affections and fruitful action, inscribed some powerful lines into the conclusion of *The Waste Land*. *The Waste Land*, 1922, is a poetic collage of lost souls and unhealthy society that, in its allusions, ranges all over world literature. It has baffled but also engrossed readers since its appearance. Here and there, in the panorama of futility, we find the poet asking whether renewal and reintegration are at all possible. His text answers its yes at the end, introduced sharply with this phrase of surprise: "Then spoke the thunder." The answer comes with three Sanskrit words from one of the Upanishads, the sacred hymns of India. The words all derive from the Indo-European root *da*, "to give." The first is *datta*.

> *Datta: what have we given?*
> *My friend, blood shaking my heart*
> *The awful daring of a moment's surrender*
> *Which an age of prudence can never retract*
> *By this, and this only, we have existed*
> *Which is not to be found in our obituaries*
> *Or in memories draped by the beneficent spider*
> *Or under seals broken by the lean solicitor*
> *In our empty rooms*

Here in *The Waste Land*, Eliot does not at all seem to be writing autobiographically, yet he was always drawing on intense experience of his own. He could well be reflecting here on his marriage to Vivienne Haigh-Wood, the most daring and impulsive move of his life. It happened in London, at a period of his recoiling from academic earnestness, when he ventured to cut loose from his native propriety. The marriage was born of his sudden attraction to a smart and flamboyant woman, very un-English for her frank but unpredictable behavior. The aftermath cost them both dearly, including Vivienne's dependency on addictive medicines and eventual confinement for mental illness. (See *T. S. Eliot, An Imperfect Life*, by Lyndall Gordon.)

Eliot faced the mess made by his unwise decision as long and as responsibly as he could. Given the rashness of his leap, why quote these words about generous self-surrender as the one hope for humanity? Because the words remain very true, very challenging. The fact that a commitment can be costly is part of its definition. That it can be unwise is a call always for the virtue of prudence—prudence not as exaggerated caution (what Eliot calls "an age of prudence") but as a careful assessment (see Chapter Seven). Adventure, casting off into the deep, is a key ingredient of a full life.

When Hope Kicks In

Eliot's words quoted from *The Waste Land* refer to moments of generous self-surrender as the one hope for humanity. The fading of optimism can be the moment for hope to kick in. This was the message smuggled out of jail and later harped upon in his writings by the Vietnamese cardinal, Francis Xavier Nguyen Van Thuan. His books *Testimony of Hope*, *The Road of Hope*, and *Prayers of Hope* all circle around this one assertion.

The same message comes from a more secular source, the hematologist and oncologist Jerome Groopman, in his provocative book, *The Anatomy of Hope: How People Prevail in the Face of Illness*. He recounts in detail a handful of his cases, some of them shadowed by failures to hope and others brightened by the opposite. Groopman acknowledges the big obstacles and deep pitfalls along the way. He begins with a definition of hope that puts it beyond starry-eyed expectation. "Hope does not arise from being told to think positively....Hope is the elevating feeling we experience when we see—in the mind's eye—a path to a better future."

I find a weakness in Groopman's final sentence above. "Elevating feeling" does not do justice to the sturdiness of real hope, which has a firm grounding that can carry it through dark nights and desperation. Whatever is going on, hope says, something is at work for the good. Saint Paul put it very directly: "We know that all things work for good for those who love God, who are called according to his purpose" (Romans 8:28). We are all called according to God's purpose. The whole world is.

Gabriel Marcel, Philosopher of Hope

The French philosopher Gabriel Marcel made hope a cornerstone of his philosophy, as appears in his collection of lectures, *Homo Viator* (*Man the Traveler*), translated by Emma Craufurd. In the preface, he discusses a character from the series of novels by Marcel Proust. The man has to admit that although there is no reason on earth for us to feel obliged "to do good, to be polite, even to be tactful," yet these impulses, these obligations, act like unknown laws within us. They "seem to belong to a different world founded on kindness, scruples, sacrifice," and we bear their teaching "without knowing who had taught us." Marcel marvels that Proust, so skeptical and prone to nihilism, could yet recognize "the existence of fixed stars in the heaven of the soul." Hope is the brightest of these stars.

Lecturing on hope to Jesuit seminarians in the darkest days of World War II, Marcel claims that hope, as a human phenomenon, arises precisely in the time of trial as "our being's veritable response" ("Sketch of a Phenomenology and a Metaphysic of Hope"). "The soul always turns towards a light which it does not yet perceive, a light yet to be born, in the hope of being delivered from its present darkness." There's something paradoxical here, he says. Those who experience life as a kind of captivity, particularly prisoners, can become the people most full of this mysterious quality, hope. "Perhaps," Marcel ventures, "hope coincides with the spiritual principle itself."

Hope is not optimism, which keeps a certain distance from things and thus "allows contradictions to be fused into a general harmony." No, Marcel says, " 'I hope' can never be taken to imply a superior vantage point....In the true character of hope, there is a lot of humility, of timidity, of chastity."

In that modest but persistent attitude, there is no room for presumption. Think of the cohort of people today fighting world hunger, AIDS, corruption in high places. They do not proceed with "high hopes" of success so much as the persuasion that a power is at work leading them and working with them. People like the Doctors Without Borders just have to do what they do. They must sense that the future is with them, if remotely. Many of them may not be believers, but something from a hidden source impels them. It must be one of "those fixed stars in the heaven of the soul." And Marcel adds, "Hope cannot be judged or ruled out on the basis of established experience. Hope is an adventure, a process of weaving experience."

The hidden process of hope does not allow impatience with results. Says Marcel, "There's a secret affinity between hope and relaxation." What we have to do is place our confidence "in a certain process of growth and development." This sounds very much like that parable of the kingdom, where the seed sprouts and grows, night and day, while the farmer idles or sleeps (Mark 4:26–9).

True long-term hope consists in "setting no condition or limit and abandoning oneself in utter confidence." The unexpected can readily happen. "One cannot say that hope sees what is going to happen; but affirms as if it saw."

We have to think about hope in interpersonal terms, Marcel insists. There is no question of one's rights to something. The right analogy is to someone "awaiting a gift or favor from another being, but only on the grounds of his liberality." We are now at the core of Marcel's teaching on hope, and we see how it applies to commitments like marriage and religious vocation. " 'I hope in thee for us'; such is perhaps the most adequate and the most elaborate expression of the act which the verb 'to hope' suggests in a way which is still confused and ambiguous." In many circumstances, the "thou" may not be very obvious, but persistent reflection will show us the "Thou" that in some way guarantees the union that holds us together. One phrase from Marcel sums it up wonderfully:

"I hope in you for us." This phrase has been a real mantra for me in my vocation, and I have done my best to pass it along to couples as they prepare for marriage.

Hope is gratuitous, Marcel reminds us again; its "centre remains beyond our reach, in those realms where values are divine gifts." Hope also demands cooperation from us, the positive contribution of our goodwill.

> At the root of hope there is something which is literally offered to us: but we can refuse hope just as we can refuse love....To live in hope is to obtain from oneself that one should remain faithful in the hour of darkness to that which in its origin was perhaps only an inspiration, an exaltation, a transport.

"What, Me Worry?"

hope in you for us." How happy I was to hear those words when Gabriel Marcel himself lectured at Louvain University shortly before my ordination in Belgium. I needed bolstering. I had spent a dozen or so years of religious life trying to be ultra-observant of what the Church and my religious order expected of me, for love of God, but with extreme anxiety. The condition is called scruples, and it can leave one's conscience, or one's psyche, with little peace. I think only my sense of humor, derived from my father, and some residue of common sense, thanks to my mother, carried me through those times. During the late fifties, *Mad Magazine* created a character named Alfred E. Newman, with the mocking caption, "What, me worry?!" When I taught high school during my years of Jesuit formation, I once overheard (or thought I overheard!) a student pinning that phrase on me. I had earned it, at any rate.

What really carried me along was devotion to the Sacred Heart of Jesus, the divine mercy embodied, especially on the cross. My novitiate reading had also conveyed some awareness of the resurrection of Christ as all pervasive, all-empowering. That awareness deepened during my theology studies, thanks to a pair of new texts in scriptural theology by Lucien Cerfaux and Francis X. Durrwell.

So here I was on the brink of ordination in 1961. I should have been overjoyed, which in many ways I was. Still, with the prospects before me of confessions and counseling and preaching, I was all too conscious of being naïve about the realities of life, especially those having to do with sexuality and with money. That may not have changed appreciably over the years, but at least it has changed some! And then there was the Mass, the holy Eucharist. How could I ever come to the holy sacrifice worthily and without awful anxiety? Equivalents of the phrase, "How should I presume?" kept rattling in my mind.

When I went before the bishop for ordination, I cannot claim that there had been any great clearing of the skies, but my spiritual director had helped me and I knew in my heart of hearts that this was where I was called. All the rest was static, which continued afterwards but gradually diminished. This mysterious life was what God called me to, invited me to. When they called out my name early in the ceremony, I could reply, "*Adsum*," ("I'm present"), along with my classmates.

Spiritually I have had to focus on confidence in God—the kind of confidence encouraged over and over in the Psalms and in the teaching of Jesus. "Cast your care upon the Lord, who will give you support" (Psalm 55:23). "O you of little faith, why did you doubt?" (Matthew 15:31). "O Sacred Heart of Jesus, I place my trust in you." Those were my mantras.

The Hopeful Council

I have left out one crucial factor, the Second Vatican Council, which opened the year after my ordination. Pope John XXIII announced its purpose as *Aggiornamento*, bringing up to date. Our teachers in Belgium had prepared us well. In Rome, after initial struggles and maneuvers over what perspective was to emerge—an outlook grounded in the Council of Trent and the classic manuals of theology or the outlook of the great theologians of the post-World War II era—the latter imposed itself.

What a breath of fresh air the Second Vatican Council was, what an instigation of hope! The Church took on a new emphasis as "the people of God." The liturgy was reshaped in line with its ancient origins and allowed to be phrased in modern languages. Religious congregations were urged to return to their founding spirit as well as to test out in what ways the daily order, "the long black line," needed modifying. Attitudes and relations to the Jews turned more positive and the outlines of ecumenism emerged. Union of church and state was displaced as a political ideal.

All of this spiritual élan coalesced into a far-reaching decree, *Gaudium et Spes* ("Joy and Hope"), also known as "The Church in the Modern World." Its opening words, quoted earlier in Chapter Four, were truly a tocsin of hope, and they continue as such, despite much subsequent dousing of the heady optimism with which the Council was received and put into effect.

Living in the Divine Milieu

During the years of the Vatican Council, which were followed by turbulent years for the world—student and liberation movements, violence, and assassinations—the spirit of hopefulness found an echo in the posthumous writings of the Jesuit, Pierre Teilhard de Chardin. Pere Teilhard, the paleontologist, made his mark among thoughtful and scientific readers with *The*

Phenomenon of Man, a set of observations about the unifying spirit at work in the natural world and in the human community.

Teilhard's truest and boldest voice comes out in his text meant for people sharing his Christian faith, *Le Milieu Divin* (*The Divine Milieu*). The title itself makes a claim that the entire earth is the scene of God's pervasive action. The earth, Teilhard points out, is the theater for an enormous human effort now underway; but the effort can easily remain self-enclosed, because Christianity has tended to steer its members around the things of this world and towards heaven. Those intent on secular pursuits, especially scientists, Teilhard says, often accuse those Catholics who work with them of giving only "a demi-effort, without feeling the spur or the inebriation of the Kingdom of God to be promoted from within human domains."

Teilhard is stressing "the possibilities and divine exigencies of every human undertaking." He teaches what Saint Francis de Sales and, in fact, Saint Paul, had insisted on long before him, the constructive value in Christ Jesus of every occupation we follow and every little thing we do. "Whether you eat or drink, or whatever you do, do everything for the glory of God" (1 Corinthians 10:31). Teilhard's is a spirituality of activism, but one where God exerts a power of transformation upon us. God does so in the times of diminishment too, when we are "passive in the hands of great unknown forces."

De Chardin sees the all-powerful Jesus, the *Pantokrator* of Greek and Russian mosaics and icons, active in our universe "through a network of organizing powers of the Total Christ." This is something, he says, "we must recognize with a flash of joy." The most transformative of these forces is the holy Eucharist. He assures us that under this "divine influence, the real Presence of the Incarnate Word, random chance gets directed, success takes on an incorruptible fullness, sorrow becomes a visit and a caress of God."

How many of us, Father Teilhard asks, "really thrill, in the depths of our heart, at the mad hope of the refashioning of our earth?" We are under no illusions of the immortality of the present earth, or of warding off most of its griefs and tears, yet we are extending ourselves together to assure "a body worthy of resurrection." What doubt can remain about why Pierre Teilhard de Chardin is considered such a beacon of hope? Almost every sentence of *The Divine Milieu* ends up urging and encouraging the reader to commitment for the kingdom of God.

As one lives, so one dies, often enough. How fitting it was that on Easter Sunday of 1955, de Chardin made his confession and celebrated the feast with the Jesuits on 93rd Street, New York City, then went home to his apartment, where he was suddenly stricken and called to God. There were 364 other days in that year, but he was called to die on the feast of hope.

A World Saved by Hope

The picture of the Church and of the world has in many ways brightened and in some major ways dimmed since the release of Teilhard's writings. Hope has not become any less crucial or any less difficult for modern men and women to live by. We are reminded of that by the second encyclical letter or treatise, *Spe Salvi* ("Saved in Hope"), addressed to the Church and the world by Pope Benedict XVI on November 30, 2007.

Pope Benedict strives to make clear the continuity between efforts for a good and just life here on earth and our heavenly destination, which must have priority but does not drain meaning from the former. "Present society is recognized by Christians as an exile; they belong to a new society which is the goal of their common pilgrimage and which is anticipated in the course of that pilgrimage." He calls attention to a third century sarcophagus which depicts "the figure of Christ as the true philosopher, holding the Gospel in one hand and the philosopher's traveling staff in the other."

Pope Benedict reminds us that we are on this road together. "While this community-oriented vision of the blessed life is certainly directed beyond the present world, as such it also has to do with the building up of this world." He mentions in particular how monasteries in the Benedictine tradition have always fostered "the nobility of work," and he asks with some bewilderment, "How did we arrive at this interpretation of the salvation of the soul as a flight from responsibility for the whole?"

Thus Benedict reaffirms the corporate nature of the hope we must have, that hope which has to underpin the serious commitments of everyday life. Each genuine commitment contributes in its way to the hope of the world. We must allow Benedict to conclude this chapter.

Hope in a Christian sense is always hope for others as well. It is an active hope in which we struggle to prevent things moving toward the 'perverse end.' "

We need the greater and lesser hopes that keep us going day by day. But these are not enough without the great hope, which must surpass everything else....Its foundation is the God who has a human face and who has loved us to the end....His love alone gives us the possibility of soberly persevering day by day, without ceasing to be spurred on by hope, in a world which by its very nature is imperfect.

7

And Now to Decide

Time to Jump?

A commitment is by its very nature a decision, a very big decision. The act of deciding, therefore, calls for special attention here. Whether to pick a certain college or career, accept a job offer, start a business, pop the question, enter religion or a seminary—each of these options takes clear thinking and strong desiring. And there are pitfalls everywhere, as we have seen in Chapters Three to Five.

Some people are prone to impetuous rash decisions, with disastrous consequences. In an excited or enthusiastic state, they cannot take in all the factors of an option or look ahead with any clarity. If something attracts them strongly or someone makes an appealing pitch to them, they may give short shrift to the negatives and the restraints.

Other people are just plain indecisive. A story about this has long been making the rounds. A farmer in Iowa had a burly workman who could lift and haul just about anything. One day, the farmer set the man before a load of potatoes, telling him to sort the big ones into one bin and the small ones into another. You guessed it. A few hours later the farmer came back to find the man sweating and tense, with just a few potatoes in each bin. "What's the trouble?" asked the farmer in exasperation. "It's the decisions!" the poor man exclaimed. As a "P" on the Myers-Briggs Inventory, I can see myself right there with him. How many times I go back and forth over the smallest option! Finally I do get to the point of saying, "Enough! Jump!"

Calm and good sense get many people through big choices, sometimes with the help of aphorisms. "Look before you leap." This is a caution light for the rash. "Fish or cut bait!" The indecisive may need a good push from something this earthy. But folk sayings can only go so far. The important thing is for people to have access to a spelled-out wisdom that could be of real help to them.

Discerning the Spirit

The Catholic Church has a spelled-out wisdom, a long history of what is called "discernment of spirits." This is based on the persuasion that a range of interior spirits move us, many originating from ourselves, but many also from benign or malicious forces outside ourselves. "The devil made me do it!" is not just a humorous excuse. There is abundant evidence and basis for it.

As Michael Buckley, SJ, puts it, "Religious experience is always an ambiguous reality" ("Discernment of Spirits," *The New Dictionary of Catholic Spirituality*). Christians of the earliest era discovered this, so great care was given to "testing the spirit," as we read in First Thessalonians (5:19–22), the earliest text in the New Testament: "Do not quench the Spirit. Do not despise prophetic utterances. Test everything; retain what is good" (5:19–21). Similarly, the First Letter of John warns those in the writer's community, "Beloved, do not trust every spirit but test the spirits to see whether they belong to God" (4:1).

The Letters of Saint Paul certainly do not make light of spirit-world influences. In Romans, Paul famously describes the battle in himself between contrary forces, "the flesh" and "the spirit."

He draws a sharp line between the two. "I discover the principle that when I want to do right, evil is at hand" (7:21). Paul issues the challenge to the community: "Discern what is the will of God, what is good and pleasing and perfect" (12:2). To the Galatians, Paul insists that they be "led by the Spirit," the Holy Spirit (Galatians 5:16–25).

Indeed the four Gospels and especially the Acts of the Apostles refer to the energizing force of the Spirit at every turn. Jesus was "led by the Spirit" into his public life. As for Acts, some scholars have dubbed them the "Acts of the Holy Spirit." The clear message of these foundational texts is that we, too, while interpreting our world, and above all, when committing ourselves to some course of action in it, must be led by the Spirit.

Letting ourselves be led by the Spirit presupposes that we can tell which way we are being impelled and, often enough, whether the impelling force is really the Spirit of God. Since New Testament times, the activity of doing this and the process to guide us has been called "discernment." The word for "discern" in the New Testament Greek is *dokimazein*. It connotes looking through appearances towards the reality. As Buckley puts it, "discernment of spirits" is the "capacity to discriminate among the various spiritual states that are being experienced." Today, Buckley points out, "discernment" has multiple and sometimes confusing applications, but what it always remains is "the interpretation of the religious meaning of various influences that bear upon human awareness and decisions."

The Catholic Church, to be sure, has no monopoly on discernment of spirits. Sometimes it seems quite the opposite. Moral philosophers and decision scientists and psychologists all have their wisdom to contribute: "Know thyself," from Socrates, is certainly a starting point that nobody would contest but everybody has trouble applying in their own case. The course of history is littered with people in power but deficient in self-knowledge, whose decisions have made a wreck of things. Current events can supply some of the same. Nonetheless, the Church has a long tradition, an accumulated wisdom, of interior discernment that one can readily draw on.

Making Wise Choices

Margaret Silf is one who can draw on these sources very practically. She does so in her handbook entitled, *Wise Choices*. Certain sections or elements in her book match my own convictions about what looms large in the process of choosing. One's starting point or, as she calls it, "Square One," deserves a lot of attention. Where has circumstance now placed me, at this stage of my life story? I am being asked not only what is now at stake, but what has been the soil of my upbringing, my particular bents and the shortcomings that I grew up into. This background leaves me constrained in many ways, with definite borders, but it also confers the resources I need. And it contains all my experience, which can warn me against going down certain paths but can also encourage me to take risks, if my risks have worked out well for me so far. "Know yourself," indeed.

As to pondering choices, Silf asks what values and guidelines we have learned from various teachers or "wisdom figures" in our lives. What resonates more strongly with me, however, are her reflections on intuition, or inner wisdom, which grows out of the values we hold dear. This is the "inner compass" that helps us sense when we are being true to ourselves or when, instead, a certain path doesn't feel quite right.

So let's suppose you have reached a conclusion. The obvious advice is: Move with it. Trust yourself. Of course, lingering serious doubts can be a valid reason to postpone a major life decision, but if this is really a crisis of confidence in yourself, a trusted friend or mentor can be the needed catalyst. The decision you are facing may well be one of the painful choices that could cost you a job or a friend for speaking frankly. Know that life is all about risks. And take the forward step.

Autobiography of Choices

Margaret Silf's way of stepping through decisions helps me understand some major decisions of my Jesuit life. Around the time of my ordination, I was seriously debating whether to ask my Jesuit superiors to assign me to join the Jesuits in Argentina. There was high concern among U.S. Catholics for the Church in Latin America, and some strong missionary volunteer programs like LAMP or the Saint James Society, founded by Cardinal Richard Cushing, drew generous participants. During my theology studies in Belgium, one of my good friends and fellow students, an Argentine Jesuit, encouraged me to follow that missionary impulse.

I considered the attraction to Argentina endlessly in those days from 1958 through 1962, thanks also to confreres from Bolivia, Chile, Peru, and Ecuador, whom I admired. Yet I never moved on it. Why not? I do not remember having anything as formal as a list of pros and cons to be weighted, yet I did it in my head. My inner compass was wavering. I had at that time literary aspirations, pretty much uncultivated. I felt that I needed time in special studies if I was to realize them for whatever future use.

Was this a failing in generosity on my part—a failure to make a whole-hearted offering to the Lord, come what may? Was I acting out the old scriptural concept of "rapine in the holocaust," stealing for myself what should be offered up to God? I am hardly a good judge of that. Anyway, I am not prone to the compulsion that Margaret Silf warns about, that of looking back to complain to myself, "If only! If only I had taken the leap." God's providence does not nap, whatever fork in the road we choose. Argentina in the '70s and early '80s became caught up in the pitiless military repression of an urban guerrilla movement. It swept up every least protester or critic of the government and invaded every center of social action. What followed was fierce interrogation, with torture (especially the *capucho*, or rubber hood) and often the dropping of suspects from aircraft into the sea. While spending a week in Buenos Aires in 1981, I walked the Plaza de Mayo where *las Madres de los Desaparecidos*, the Mothers of the Disappeared, marched weekly. I remember staring grimly at the Naval Headquarters at the end of the Plaza, a building notorious as a torture center.

Between 1963 and 1968, I was sent by my Jesuit province to attend the University of Michigan to study English and American Literature, so as to prepare for college teaching and interact with writers on a campus that fostered them. Those were years of worldwide ferment, peaking in 1968. In our country, the Civil Rights Movement took center stage and then shared it with the Vietnam War. The campus in Ann Arbor was swirling with anti-war protest. Our Jesuit superior general, Father Pedro Arrupe, addressed a letter to all American Jesuits, urging us to take more concentrated and conscientious action for civil rights. Our record with African-Americans had been none too glorious. Father Arrupe was emphatic about taking part in their education.

Here I was, just finishing a PhD in English, due to return to California to teach in a Jesuit University. But I was a proper candidate to take up Father Arrupe's call, available if anyone was, and I was fired up to do so. The University of Michigan had a program of collaboration with Tuskegee Institute in Alabama, one of the flagship Black colleges, and they offered to fly me down to have a look. The Dean of Arts and Sciences at Turskegee, Doctor Howard Carter, gave me a warm welcome and invited me to join them, as did the Chair of English, Doctor Youra Qualls.

I did not hesitate this time. The inner compass did not quaver, though it had some reason to. After all, I was heading into the totally unknown, shortly after the tense march on Selma. That year, 1968, the students at Tuskegee surrounded the Board of Trustees meeting in Dorothy Hall, the guest enclave, to present "unconditional demands." The National Guard arrived, and they fled.

For my part, I needed the permission of my Jesuit provincial in California to take up Tuskegee's invitation. When I wrote to him for this permission, tremulously, no surprise! He did not grant it. I had to say to myself: You started the machinery going; what do you do now? I had only one option, one I had never dreamed I would ever exercise, to write to our superior general in Rome, Father Arrupe, and ask, in effect, "Did you mean that letter?" He responded, welcoming my offer and promising to tell that to my provincial; but he made clear that the provincial, who was the superior on the scene, still had the final decision. My provincial, Father John F. X. Connolly, knew my weaknesses all too well. More than that, he was anguished by all the leakage from our membership during the turbulence of those years. Yet despite himself, he said yes.

So off I went for two years to Alabama. My one serious misgiving, the one big negative that Margaret Silf would have urged that I ponder, was fear of loneliness; but I bit the bullet. And in that conflictual and exciting time and place, loneliness was the one adventure that never occurred to me. (I wrote a pamphlet-size account of that time, "What Father Arrupe Did to Me," in *Studies in the Spirituality of Jesuits*.)

In the two cases above, I engaged in what is called discernment, but not too consciously and without benefit of the more exacting study of that process now available. The process is still, I must admit, pretty mysterious and complex to me, not so much in its abstract form, but in how it works out—above all—in our prayer.

In the late nineties, I made another big decision, after spending the decade in New York City as an editor of *America* Magazine, the national Jesuit opinion weekly. I loved New York City and the magazine, too. It was the best fit for me. So why did I choose to leave? My fellow editors judged that I wanted to get back to West Coast weather. Not really! I was nearing seventy and thought it about time to get closer to my Jesuit home base. Also, I had been covering stories in Latin America, and my energy was giving out for those trips and the scrambling about that they involved. I felt sheepish, a bit fraudulent, for writing as a two-week expert on a succession of countries, much as I had loved the chance to do so. The one assignment that might have kept me at *America*, poetry editing, was already covered. (Ironically, I now fill that very role, from three thousand miles away.) I think with a twinge still about having given up the New York assignment—hoping, I must say, that younger Jesuits would come to fill the editorial shoes. But I do not remember wrestling much with the decision, which landed me near enough to California but with another commitment that stretched me: three years of partnership with Mexican Jesuits teaching in Tijuana.

Now the question arises (and my editor at Liguori Publications puts it to me): How does my experience connect to that of anyone who might be reading these pages? My impulse is to answer: In the way that stories do. Stories happen outside our own ambiance, yet we can recognize ourselves and our world in them unmistakably sometimes. Issues come up in stories. My own contains these elements: a battle of pros and cons (attraction and resistance), a need for better self-understanding, the lack of a real mentor, the role of intuition, the readiness to risk.

Ignatius Loyola Learns Discernment

As I undertake here to speak in more general terms of discernment, that major topic in the Church and among spiritual directors these days, I turn to the one source really familiar to me, the spiritual experience and teaching of Ignatius of Loyola.

In the *Autobiography of Ignatius Loyola*, sometimes called *Reminiscences*, recorded by Luis Goncalves da Camara, SJ, we learn how the combative young courtier was forced into a long convalescence after getting his leg shattered in defense of the fortress of Pamplona in the Spanish Basque country in 1521. In the Loyola mansion, he whiled away the hours imagining ambitious feats to impress a certain young noblewoman; but he was also reading perforce the only two books in the house, a Life of Christ and a book of lives of the saints. Ignatius tells us that his mind spent hours on either the secular imaginings or the religious ones, that is, on chivalric feats to impress a lady love or on heroics of holiness in imitation of Saint Dominic or other saints. Suddenly it dawned on him how different their effect was.

> When he was thinking about that worldly stuff he would take much delight, but when he left it aside after getting tired, he would find himself dry and discontented. But when about going to Jerusalem barefoot, and about not eating except herbs, and about doing all the other rigours he was seeing the saints had done, not only used he to be consoled while in such thoughts, but he would remain content and happy even after having left them aside.
>
> SAINT IGNATIUS OF LOYOLA, PERSONAL WRITINGS
> TRANSLATED BY JOSEPH A. MUNITIZ AND PHILIP ENDEAN

Ignatius tells that "he began to marvel at this difference in kind and to reflect on it...little by little coming to know the difference in kind of spirits that were stirring: the one from the devil, and the other from God." These were "Ah-ha!" moments for Ignatius. Thus did his discernment begin, which later became so fruitful for others. Eventually he slips away from his family, who recognizes what he is drawn to and wants to prevent it, and he ends up at the town of Manresa, near Barcelona, to devote himself to prayer and penances.

At Manresa, Ignatius meets all the challenges of an unguided novice, in particular the consoling but ambiguous visions of an image in serpent form whose recurrence delights him but leaves him sad upon disappearing. He later realizes clearly that this was not from God or for his good. Thus in his Spiritual Exercises, which he began composing during the Manresa and Barcelona years, he would say for us to keep an eye on the outcome, the residue, of our exalted impressions to see what spirit, perhaps fallacious, is at work and whether it is genuinely from God.

Ignatius had abundant consolation in his prayer at Manresa, and one extraordinary vision that marked his understanding of the faith and of the spiritual path for life. But he also had a full experience of spiritual conflict. There was, for example, his battle with discouragement, the nagging thought, "How are you going to be able to stand this life the seventy years you're meant to live?" This falls into the "What if?" category explained by Margaret Silf. One gets to asking oneself, "What if a, b, or c were to occur during the course of my commitment; how can I possibly be true to it?" Ignatius, sensing this thought was from the enemy, responded with great force, "You wretch! Can you promise me one hour of life?"

Ignatius also underwent dryness of spirit, sadness and desolation at Manresa, and terrible scruples (endless worrying about details of his religious observance and whether he had well confessed his past sins). He was tempted at times to throw himself in desperation out of the window of the upper-story room. Then one day, as he tells it, "the Lord willed that he woke up as from sleep." No more going back over his past in confession, no more excesses in penance (severely curtailing sleep, avoiding meat, etc.).

Ignatius was now more and more habitually sifting whether the good spirit or a harmful spirit was impelling his attitudes and decisions. As he recalled later, "At this time, God was dealing with him in the same way as a schoolteacher deals with a child, teaching him." And at this time, Ignatius himself, as a spiritual novice, starts organizing in his precious notebook what he had learned and offering help to other wayfaring souls. In his Spiritual Exercises, given its initial form in Barcelona after his return from pilgrimage to the Holy Land, Ignatius devotes much space and care to what he entitles, "The Making of an Election." Election, the big decision, is of course what kicks off a major commitment. The Exercises, to a major degree, are focused to this point: What will you now do with your life? What should you do?

The Three Times for Choice

All big choices, Ignatius reminds us, have to be between acceptable alternatives—nothing harmful to oneself or others or opposed to Church teaching. Ignatius, on his way to Montserrat and his change of life, fell into conversation with a Muslim who spoke of Our Lady in ways seeming to disparage her. Still a courtier at heart, Ignatius debated whether he should follow after the man and stab him to vindicate Mary's honor. Not an acceptable alternative! Ignatius could not decide and, at a fork in the road, let his mule pick whether to follow the Moor's path. The beast had sense enough not to!

Ignatius proposes "Three Times, Each of them Suitable for Making a Sound and Good Election." The first time is when a possible way of action hits you with the certainty, "This is it!" One is lightning-struck, just as the young Saul on his way to Damascus was blinded by the light, just as Matthew at his money table was called away by the compelling voice, "Follow me." We hear of this happening in romance from time to time. At a silver or wedding anniversary, for instance, one of the spouses will confess, "The moment I met her (or him), I knew right away that this was the one."

"The Second Time," the Exercises say, happens "when sufficient clarity and knowledge are received from the experience of consolations and desolations, and from experience in the discernment of various spirits" (The Institute of Jesuit Sources, St. Louis, translated by George E. Ganss, SJ). We have a perfect example of that in the tremendous seesaw that Ignatius lived through during his convalescence, spontaneously moved by his reading in quite different ways until he came to reflect on where God was drawing him. Those engaged in a battle of feelings—even a turmoil of feelings—over some major choice, must realize this is no time for them to throw up their hands in despair. Rather, this is a fruitful time to tease out, with grace, where they are really being led. A mentor, a trustworthy guide, can be crucial in this process. And this clearly must not be someone who enjoys making decisions for other people!

The Third Time, Ignatius says, is one of tranquility. "By a time of tranquility, I mean one when the soul is not being moved one way and the other by various spirits and uses its natural faculties in freedom and peace." He points out that the true purpose of our lives—to praise God our Lord and to save our souls—has to consciously govern our choice. So the question, "How can I serve God better (or best)?" has to be in the forefront. And then we proceed with a calm assessment, whether resorting to that list of pros and cons or considering what we would advise someone dear to us or imagining ourselves at death's door looking back. Ignatius helps us pray over the matter: "I should beg God our Lord to be pleased to move my will and to put into my mind what I ought to do in regard to the matter proposed so that it will be more to his praise and glory." So it is not just a practical decision we seek, but one that will lock us in closer to God's desire for us and to following, the best we can, the divine will.

Musing on the three decisions of my own that I discussed earlier in this chapter, I suddenly realized that they each fall into one of the three times. The decision about applying to be sent to Argentina falls in the second time, with consolation at the prospect but much uncertainty nevertheless. The decision in favor of Tuskegee Institute seems to belong in the first time, because the whole possibility excited me right from the start. The decision about leaving *America* Magazine, more coolly made, seems proper to the third time.

At this point, a reader could profit from thinking back to some big decision he or she has made and exploring the dynamics of it. Under which of the three times did it fall? The reader facing a big decision in the present, a possible commitment, might well ask the same thing, remembering that each of these states may have its counterfeit. Infatuation or rash enthusiasm can mask as the lightning strike of the first time. What the old spiritual masters called abulia, temperamental indecisiveness, can stretch out the second time endlessly (as it did for me). And a kind of super-rationality, or scorn of feelings, can be lurking in the third time.

An Attitude of Indifference

For Ignatius, the doorway, the real entryway to discernment and the big decisions, lies in his teaching on "indifference." He introduces this term at the outset of the Spiritual Exercises when laying the groundwork of spirituality, in a brief consideration called "Principle and Foundation." Here he spells out for us as retreatants, quite succinctly, what we exist for before God and what attitude should guide us always. Everything about us on earth, he says, is created for us to help achieve our purpose, which is "to serve, reverence and serve Christ our Lord, and thereby to save our souls."

> To attain this it is necessary to make ourselves indifferent to all created things, in regard to everything which is left to our free will and is not forbidden. Consequently, on our part, we ought not to seek health rather than sickness, wealth rather than poverty, honor rather than dishonor, a long life rather than a short one, and so on in all other matters.
>
> Rather, we ought to desire and choose only that which is more conducive to the end for which we are created.

The "Principle and Foundation" ends right there. What Ignatius means by the phrase "indifference" is quite other than the lazy, non-caring attitude commonly evoked by that word. Young people communicate this indifference by saying, "Whatever," with a shrug, meaning, "It doesn't really matter." Or they may even mean, "Nothing really matters." The sense of Ignatius is quite opposite. We are to stay acutely tuned to the divine influence, ready to be moved at a breath. Energy and enthusiasm may well then move us, as it did Mary replying to the angel: "I am the handmaid of the Lord, be it done to me according to your message." Incidentally, if the above phrasing in the "Principle and Foundation" sounds a lot like the marriage vows, well, isn't that the spirit of those vows?

A Freewill Offering

To conclude, there are people who believe that our course in life is fated. Willy-nilly, our choices are preset. Forces beyond us, including God's will, somehow determine not just what will happen to us but what we do. Saint Ignatius, despite his tremendous sense of God's governance and creative will, would have none of that. God's grace does not overpower anyone. We have an irreplaceable role in giving form to our lives. Ignatius was a thorough believer in human freedom.

Ignatius lived during the Renaissance and Reformation, where the relative roles of grace and free will were hotly debated between Catholics and Reformers. Ignatius was definitely on the side of free will, that is, wise choice, as our true calling. It is what God calls us to and invites us to via the Holy Spirit. Thus commitment played a central part in his view of the desirable response of the human creature to God. Ignatius would agree completely with Thomas More speaking to Richard Rich in the play and movie, *Man for All Seasons*. We hold our soul preciously in our hands like water, and if, with some betrayal, we open our fingers and let it slip through, we cannot get it back. Yes, you are right, Ignatius would also say to Marcel Lieberman. It is in the main choices we make that we gain self-understanding; we find out who we are.

We find this great respect for a person's free and earnest choice—in other words, a person's commitment—in the prayers of the Spiritual Exercises. His meditation, "The Kingdom of Christ," culminates in an offering of oneself as of a knightly vassal kneeling before a throne.

Eternal Lord of all things, I make my offering, with your favor and help. I make it in the presence of your infinite Goodness, and of your glorious Mother, and of all the holy men and women in your heavenly court. I wish and desire, and it is my deliberate decision, provided only that it is for your greater service and praise, to imitate you in bearing all injuries and affronts, and any poverty, actual as well as spiritual, if your Most Holy Majesty desires to choose and receive me into such a life and state.

Saint Ignatius is credited also, though without verification, with a Prayer for Generosity, opening, "Dear Lord, teach me to be generous." It certainly is in the spirit of the prayer above. Finally, we have the concluding prayer of the Spiritual Exercises, now so well known and cherished. It is the focal point of the "Contemplation to Attain Love."

> Take, Lord, and receive all my liberty, my memory, my understanding, and all my will—all that I have and possess. You, Lord, have given all that to me. I now give it back to you, O Lord. All of it is yours. Dispose of it according to your will. Give me love of yourself along with your grace, for that is enough for me.

The key phrase above is "receive all my liberty." We are not giving it up, annihilating it, but instead dedicating it, activating it completely. The last word in this matter of Christian commitment, that is, in the well-focused exercise of our human faculties, must go to Saint Gregory of Nyssa, one of the early Fathers of the Church. "We are in a sense our own parents, and we give birth to ourselves by our own free choice of what is good. Such a choice becomes possible for us when we have received God into ourselves and have become children of God, children of the Most High." To give birth to ourselves is to give ourselves a genuine identity, which is what a commitment makes possible. We then know we are someone. And we can do this, in the last analysis, by the baptismal grace whereby "for freedom Christ set us free" (Galatians 5:1).

8

Sailing the Rough Waters

Going Long Distance

A commitment is not a hundred-yard dash; often enough it is a marathon. In the world of track and field, the long-distance runners follow very different imperatives of breathing, leg muscle development, conditioning, and timing than do the speedsters. The sprinter has to be explosive, summoning great physical input right off the block. The marathoner has to pace himself or herself, thinking of the long haul, not straining, not dehydrating, keeping up with the core runners while waiting to make the big move.

During my forties and fifties I took to running, though hardly in competition, and I loved it. Later, living in New York City during the nineties, I would try to catch the end of the New York Marathon for the thrill of seeing the leaders surge into view and then come swinging into Central Park, with Kenyans and Ethiopians always in evidence. But the two images that linger with me are of the women's Olympics. In 2008, with African women hot in pursuit, a Romanian, Constantina Tomescu-Dita, took the lead after about an hour and just stayed there, loping along well ahead, right into the stadium in Beijing. Neither among race horses nor among humans can the front runner often manage that. Other Olympics watchers found it boring, but for me it was exhilarating.

My other image is from the 1984 Olympics in Los Angeles, but not of Joan Beloit from Maine, the decisive winner. No, the image is of a Swiss runner, Gabriela Andersen-Schiess, dehydrated and dazed, dragging herself across the finish line as if ready to drop, to end up in thirty-seventh place. If the first image is of confidence and strength, cruising along, the second is of determination and courage, sheer grit. Both images are appropriate to commitment over the long course, whether for extended human service, a demanding profession, maintenance of shaky health, tending a family member, marriage vows, religious dedication, some long-term project of research or art. We can profit from both these contrasting images, for who hasn't, at some time or other, been the exhausted Swiss runner?

Shakespeare, that peerless observer of our follies and finer moments, was able to catch the episodes of stumbling and tripping up in the running of human lives. His string of romantic comedies— *Much Ado about Nothing*, *As You Like It*, *Twelfth Night*, etc.—are summed up in one pithy reflection at the start of *A Midsummer Night's Dream*: "The course of true love never did run smooth." We know too that Shakespeare, in his comedies, after he takes his lovers through their obstacle courses, ends them up at the altar. He leaves them there as if all will infallibly be well thereafter.

One thing we know about romance is that all will not infallibly be well thereafter. The Shakespearean newlyweds, Beatrice and Benedict, will again take to ragging at each other, and the shrew, Kate, will not keep up her mousy submission to Petruchio for long, and the Jew and Gentile, Jessica and Lorenzo, will have a far from easy time of it in Venice. A whole new set of episodes in the domestic drama can be expected, and so with other commitments as well. The purpose of this final chapter is to discuss that phenomenon of stresses and crisis moments of the commitment.

Some Bucking Up From Saint Paul

Saint Paul, in the various letters we have under his name, keeps encouraging renewal of commitment and faithfulness. The young bishop Timothy, for instance, was Paul's right-hand man, but his spirits must have been flagging when the apostle had to admonish him, "I remind you to stir into flame the gift of God that you have through the imposition of my hands. For God did not give us a spirit of cowardice but rather of power and love and self-control. So do not be ashamed of your testimony to our Lord" (2 Timothy 1:6–8). Evodia and Syntyche, valued collaborators with Paul, seem to have gotten in each other's hair, to the harm of the ministry, and needed to hear these chiding words: "I urge Evodia and I urge Syntyche to come to a mutual understanding in the Lord" (Philippians 4:2). And Paul is severe with the little community of Corinthians for letting lawsuits arise among them: "Can it be that there is not one among you wise enough to be able to settle a case between brothers?" (1 Corinthians 6:5).

Bearing with one another is a frequent theme with Paul. He sounds it to those favorites of his, the Philippians, reminding them of the extraordinary humbleness of Christ and drawing the lesson for them: "Complete my joy by being of the same mind, united in heart, thinking one thing....Humbly regard others as better than yourselves" (2:2–3). He puts it memorably in the passage about genuine love in First Corinthians: "It bears all things, believes all things, hopes all things, endures all things" (13:7). He exhorts the Galatians: "Bear one another's burdens, and so you will fulfill the law of Christ" (6:2). And to the Colossians he gives the full picture of how one should live in community, including the marriage community:

Put on then, as God's chosen ones, holy and beloved, heartfelt compassion, kindness, humility, gentleness, and patience, bearing with one another and forgiving one another, if one has a grievance against another; as the Lord has forgiven you, so must you also do (Colossians 3:12–13).

We are all too conscious of Paul having instructed wives, "Be subordinate to your husbands, as is proper in the Lord," but we pay less attention to the crucial words that follow: "Husbands, love your wives, and avoid any bitterness toward them....Fathers, do not provoke your children, so they may not become discouraged" (Colossians 3:18–21). Among Christians, when the marital commitment runs into trouble, it is not for lack of steering from Saint Paul. Bitterness, carping, argument, irritability, and what we call "long memory" is grist for the devil's mill, no doubt about it. The Letter to the Hebrews too makes that perfectly clear: "See to it that no one be deprived of the grace of God, that no bitter root spring up and cause trouble, through which many may become defiled" (12:15). And through bitterness, we may add, many commitments come to grief.

A commitment between two parties, whether it be a business partnership or a marriage or something else, is calculated to mature the two parties. And if the commitment be to a worthy cause or to a vocation, it again has the virtue of stretching or maturing the individual. Self-understanding deepens in the process; if it doesn't, the whole project is at risk. Saint Paul regards this as a matter of passing from the condition of fleshly people, "infants in Christ" (1 Corinthians 3:1), "tossed by waves" (Ephesians 4:14), to more solidity of character and more "mature manhood." By "mature manhood," he does not imply anything about gender but rather about "the full stature of Christ" (Ephesians 4:13). In brief, a reading and rereading of Saint Paul yields precious and full instructions on living out the Christian commitment. As he tells the Galatians, summing up his whole letter to them: "For freedom Christ set us free" (5:1). Our baptism, our initial commitment, sets us on the path; then we must make our way, advancing on it.

Our human freedom receives the constant strengthening called grace, and if we allow it to do so, blessed are we. We could not well proceed with our own commitments if we did not have positive examples and the witness of those we admire. Anniversaries are often when this happens, though we know that the occasions tend to gloss over frictions and scars, past and present; the coloring tends toward rose. For Shakespeare was right; the course of authentic love does not run swimmingly. Rapids and unseen rocks may throw into peril the whole enterprise. The cross will mark each of our joint or solitary endeavors unavoidably.

Anniversaries and jubilees are not occasions to crow, really, so much as times to lift the heart in thanks. They make possible a long look backward in gratitude, but just as helpfully offer a chance for renewal of spirit. The yearly anniversary of wedding or ordination is less dramatic but affords an even more practical, because more frequent, opportunity (or *kairos*) to rekindle the spirit. Saint Paul urges the Corinthians not to delay their reconciliation with God and with one another: "Behold, now is a very acceptable time, now is the day of salvation" (2 Corinthians 6:2).

Staying On Course

The wisdom books of the Old Testament have their say about hewing to the Lord against forces pushing us off the path. Many of these passages locate us right beside the Hebrew students in a rabbinical school. The movie, *Yentl*, featuring Barbra Streisand, reminds us of how highly male this environment was, since Yentl, with her great yearning for Jewish wisdom, had to disguise herself to enter it.

My son, when you come to serve the Lord,
    prepare yourself for trials.
Be sincere of heart and steadfast,
    undisturbed in time of adversity.
Cling to him, forsake him not;
    thus will your future be great.
Accept whatever befalls you,
    in crushing misfortune be patient;
For in fire gold is tested,
    and worthy men in the crucible of humiliation.
Trust God and he will help you;
    make straight your ways and hope in him.

THE WISDOM OF SIRACH 2:1–6

Margaret Silf devotes the final pages of *Wise Choices* to discussing what to do when our enduring choices fall upon hard times. What to do, she asks, when the inner compass wavers? In her last few pages, she reminds us it is liberating to realize we cannot change the past.

Saint Ignatius had his own way of saying this, in the "Rules for Discernment of Spirits for Week 1" of the Spiritual Exercises. He is talking about commitment to the spiritual life, where the two guideposts are consolation and desolation. For him, desolation includes "obtuseness of soul, turmoil within it, an impulse toward low and earthly things, or disquiet from various agitations and temptations." Ignatius comments: "These move one toward lack of faith and leave one without hope and without love. One is completely listless, tepid, and unhappy, and feels separated from our Creator and Lord."

Outstanding religious people, like Saint Thérèse of Lisieux and Mother Teresa of Calcutta, have gone through extreme and long-lasting desolation, deprived of its polar opposite, "abundant fervor, augmented love, and intensive grace." They nonetheless remained faithful to what Ignatius advises: "During a time of desolation, one should not make a change. Instead, one should remain firm and constant in the resolutions and in the decision which one had on the day before the desolation." Of course, Ignatius adds, "it is profitable for us to make vigorous changes in ourselves against the desolation," especially if we have grown lax or negligent or opened the door to a harmful spirit in some way. Examine yourself, meditate, maybe take on some penance (as we do in Lent), he tells us.

As a confessor and counselor, I perceive at times that when someone is miserable not really by their own fault, as in an unhappy marriage, the condition itself is penance enough. I have been astonished, edified, made anxious—all at the same time—by how much certain women have to put up with from an unfaithful, addicted, or abusive spouse and yet go on fighting to keep the promise they made before God. I see this so often in Hispanic ministry, which I have been conducting in parishes. Those that can so endure deserve the commendation from the Psalms: "Whoever keeps an oath despite the cost…shall never be shaken" (Psalm 15:4–5). I say this advisedly, because there is much shaking of the head nowadays about some who stay in dysfunctional relationships, as if they are offending their own dignity and contributing to dysfunction. Sometimes they are, no doubt, but sometimes, following their own lights, they truly deserve credit.

To Stay or Not to Stay With the Ship

These determined spouses, driven to distraction often enough, have been faithful to the Catholic tradition, as Ignatius reflects it when discussing matters of election: "Some matters fall under the heading of an unchangeable election, such as priesthood, marriage, and the like." Nonetheless, one has to worry instinctively, especially about the abusive marriage: "When is enough enough?" and to ask dubiously, "Can this marriage be restored?"

Not all commitments are so "unchangeable," but even with these others, stability and continuity are of the essence. The advice of Ignatius to hold tight, not to go into reverse right away when in the dark or bottoming out, can be a lifeline. Eventually, in a calmer moment, with some time taken to achieve perspective, the counsel of Margaret Silf deserves attention. She tells us that if we've made a bad choice, it may be necessary to make a change, if we have the courage and no one will be hurt by it.

I look back now on words that I wrote a quarter century ago and find them still apropos.

> These days, late in the twentieth century, give us the frequent spectacle of people coming to their senses, beginning to straighten out, far down the road of their lives. Second careers often mean that people find themselves first after painfully switching direction; so do some second marriages, or the return to secular life from religious orders. Considering the fallout, the hurt to others and occasional wreckage that the second chance often entails, it does not, as a solution, satisfy as fully as the rediscovery of a first love. But it is a solution, often the only one; sometimes it is the originally right one asserting itself.
>
> A person should be happy and feel privileged, no matter at what advanced date, to have gained some stability, learned to give and take, "mellowed out." The Catholic Church, in its approach to dispensations and annulments, has come, if slowly, to recognize this, even while struggling to keep the sights clear and not to play fast and loose with serious commitments.
>
> "Coming to Reason," *Human Development*

I referred to sacramental marriage, priesthood, and religious vows earlier as the "unchangeables." People of the postmodern era will squint in puzzlement at such a concept. The commitment in a sacramental marriage "till death," the vow or promise of celibacy—how countercultural they are. Our contemporaries will shake their heads in disapproval of being thus tied down. Those who accept and believe in such dedication have to look to their moorings constantly in such skeptical company. Social creatures as we are, we cannot escape being affected by others.

The political and cultural turmoil of the late 1960s and '70s shook loose a good half of those following religious and priestly vocations. For some it was liberation from somewhere they didn't belong in the first place, for others puzzlement and discouragement in post-Vatican times, for still others the heightened attractions of intimacy. From those of us on the playing field, it was hard not to be judgmental in those times. Today, on meeting these former confreres, I find many truly at peace before God, but some who still have some "root of bitterness" about the Catholic Church or their religious order. To be unforgiving is to put oneself in the enemy's hand, the one whom Ignatius calls "the enemy of human nature." Jesus himself could not have made his message about readiness to forgive any clearer, double underlining it in the "Our Father" and devoting parables to this lesson.

I try to make my own this passage full of understanding by the late Father Bernard Häring, Redemptorist. He puts the expectations of celibacy simply and familiarly: "A person who feels called to the celibate priesthood will put all his trust in God's grace, maintain a healthy prayer life, walk wisely and keep vigilance." Helpfully too he observes "that it might become clear that celibacy is not really that person's calling." In that case, one should be lovingly encouraged to ask for a dispensation without fear of being ostracized or despised by the Church" (*Priesthood Imperiled, A Critical Examination of*

Ministry in the Catholic Church). Father Häring, theologian and moralist, recognizes that some priests "with deep human and religious qualities" have an ongoing battle to stay at peace sexually, and he advises against this being "senselessly overdramatized."

Resources for a Celibate Vocation

How can a priest, brother, or religious sister maintain a lifetime commitment that seems often to be an obstacle path? By growing in it. Resources for growth are very much at hand and must be consciously part of the choice. Daily personal prayer is resource number one. Bishop Fulton Sheen promoted and was faithful to a holy hour each day, which many priests now observe, with some reading, meditation, and the Divine Office. Religious order priests have long had daily meditation in their rule, although sticking with it has always been a challenge. Many bishops approve and encourage small chapels in the parish rectories, since a priest often cannot go into his own church without somebody approaching him.

Resources, in fact, abound for commitment to ministry. Priest support groups have kept increasing, thanks to the Jesu Caritas and Emmaus movements and others, which draw the members together monthly for prayer, for the Eucharist, and for faith sharing. The aid available in spiritual direction, long a tradition in religious orders, has been dawning gradually on everyone, with the number of trained directors—priests and religious sisters and laity—increasing also. This special ministry, a Catholic treasure, has spread into Protestant and Jewish circles as well. Much weight has always been given to the yearly retreat as a time of soul-searching and rekindling of the fire. Though socializing and even golf have cut into the effectiveness of many diocesan retreats, yet with an inspiring retreat master, this can still be the real time of grace. The individually-directed retreat, instead of a group retreat with a series of conferences, has more and more become an ideal, with personal guidance and tailored suggestion for prayer available daily.

Among priests, brothers, and women religious too, the strain on commitment has to be eased at regular times, to say nothing of aided in crises by competent help. Sabbatical programs abound, where they can catch their breath after long exertion in the ministry, absorb newer teaching, and deepen spiritually. As for those judged to be pretty much on the ropes, live-in "rediscovery" programs also exist and, despite a few sorry past histories among the initial programs, are proving their worth.

Marriage in Rough Waters

Marriage is still the principal Christian commitment. The stresses upon it, sadly, have escalated, but it was never an easy proposition. We just seem to be recognizing the odds more honestly. In *Priesthood Imperiled*, Father Häring has some helpful words. "Marriage, as understood from the prevailing perspective of grace, means trusting that God will graciously empower persons to dare to commit themselves to the marriage covenant with its promise of lifelong fidelity." Since marriage depends upon two people, however, they need concerted teamwork to get through the rough waters. Nothing can guarantee that, but churches have at least initiated a process of evaluating couples and talking turkey with them beforehand. In recent decades too, says Häring, canonists and moralists have come to recognize that quite a number of those weddings celebrated in church could be recognized as invalid, since they are sick and sickening from the start. "Although these couples are more or less normal, they [the individuals] are often in character, feeling, and other important respects so radically different as to be strangers to each other, and hence allergic to one another."

Difficulties in marriage do not commonly start with an allergy, however, though they may escalate into what seems like one. The Christian Family Movement in the middle of the last century and Marriage Encounter in more recent decades have exerted themselves to strengthen the union and renew faith. Starting in French Canada in the early '70s, yet another movement has gone further, attending to marriages that look to be on the rocks. Priests, counselors, and clinics have long dealt with this emergency situation, but now they have the help of Retrouvaille, meaning "Rediscovery," a three-month program that I was recently privileged to see in action, with eighteen couples enrolled.

Retrouvaille is, above all, a no-nonsense approach to healing miscommunication. It also labors to make clear all the areas of danger in a marital relation and how the slide into failure can take place. For the opening weekend and through six Saturday meetings in the following three months, the presentations are closely scripted and their order carefully laid out. Graduates from Retrouvaille, as panelist couples, interweave their testimonies with the prepared script, as does the clergy member always there on hand.

Participant couples in Retrouvaille do a lot of writing—notetaking, journal entries, even letters—to be shared and discussed between spouses in notebook exchanges. In the half-day session I attended, I found the topics quite substantial and the presenters admirably direct. Banners of the type familiar from Marriage Encounter hung around the hall: "Love is a Decision," "Feelings are Neither Right or Wrong," "God does not make Junk," plus one that must be particular to Retrouvaille: "The Past is past, let's begin again." The whole program is laboring to bring that final banner out of the realm of the purely wishful. I was told that judges in divorce courts sometimes send a couple to attend Retrouvaille, if they see prospects for averting the divorce. I was also told that, within the groups and among the couples, rediscovery does keep happening; the ship can be steered in off the rocks.

A Tribute to Guardians

The poet and dramatist, T.S. Eliot, who has appeared earlier in these pages, deserves to re-enter here at the conclusion. In his mature years, the years that gave us *Four Quartets*, Eliot, as playwright, wrote *The Cocktail Party*. It is set in London among adult party givers and party goers in their own social circle. It has a comic aura to animate the proceedings, due to a chatty fussbudget and a colonial inspector full of stories. And it has an aura of mystery due to an unidentified guest, who turns out in later scenes to be a psychiatrist.

The plot of *The Cocktail Party* turns upon a married couple, Edward and Lavinia, who have grown cold to each other. The wife seems to have skipped out. Her husband, who is left with hosting this entourage, has had an affair going with Celia, the young single woman present. Peter, the young man in the group, looks to the single woman with romantic yearning. It was all very contemporary in 1950 and still is.

The three characters who are not part of the problem here gradually appear as part of the solution. Julia and Alex act as catalysts to keep interaction going among the other four, and Reilly is available as a plainspoken guide to the troubled confessings. When the three eventually announce themselves as The Guardians, picking up their glasses for a libation and a special prayer for Celia, we realize they have been acting with intentionality throughout. They indeed constitute a providence for the uncertain four.

If this comes close to home for us, it should. Plenty of us will admit that such guardians, as part of an overarching providence, are what get us through the long stretch of a commitment with its ups and downs, its consolations and desolations. This has proved true in my own case certainly, and I need, on closing, to give witness to that. Whenever my heart and eyes have strayed, or my faith faltered, or my spirits flagged from some disappointment—

including my mother's death—there was always a Julia or Alex or Reilly. There was always the divine hand of the one steering. As a practical recognition of that, whenever I go out on the road, I always begin by invoking my angel guardian and Mary, Our Lady of the Way. For the above reasons, I make bold to conclude with this poem of mine.

Right there's the accident,
 dear guardian, where I ventured
onto the expressway
 too soon, too slow.
The horn came blaring by us.

More than once, thank you,
 it never happened. I tremble
for each hair-raising time,
 dear companion, dear guide,
thinking how close a call.

And so this year come shocks
 inevitable: young driver
into me, me into one unseen.
 Crash! Crunch!
Yet we all walk away.

Got to believe you,
 angel, hand upon mine,
steering the steerer,
 our way long, long,
you not for a second dazed.

To Sum It Up

My original title for this book was *Commitment? You Must Be Kidding!* The phrase has some spark, I think, but may not strike a very positive note, and it was dropped. The mock incredulity of those words do, however, mirror my concern over a young-adult culture today very dubious about commitment. I have tried to explore what the undermining factors are. Above all, however, I have wanted to share my own sense of how crucial commitments still are and my own story about the role they have played in my life and in the lives of those around me.

For many years, after some bewildering or amusing encounter, I have found myself resorting wryly to the old exclamation, "It's a great life!" And it is. Each of our days is unpredictable, full of hazards, crises, pratfalls, dark passages, but also full of bright moments and wonderful coincidence. Commitments are what have made my life worthwhile—the commitments of my parents to me, and of the Society of Jesus to me, and, reciprocally, my own major and minor commitments along the way—to good writing and literature, to the Latinos in our churches, to a variety of dear friends. Reader, I wish and pray something the same for you.

ACKNOWLEDGMENTS

Dare to Commit: Say Yes in a World of Maybe came about by happy fault—what in Latin is called *felix culpa*. Liguori Publications had invited me to undertake something quite different, but my mishandling of my message system kept their inquiry from reaching me until much too late. Liguori kindly gave me a second chance to explore and try to counteract the rarity and great difficulty of commitment in modern life.

Certain people played a key role in my pursuit of this crucial but slippery topic. Father John Stoeger of the Archdiocese of Los Angeles, in particular, thanks to his long experience with spiritual direction and parish discussion groups, urged me on from the start and was an astute reader of early drafts. I received early encouragement also from three Jesuit confreres: Fathers John D. Murphy, Marc Roselli, and Bernard Bush. Finally, I was blessed with careful readings by a good friend, Henry A. Foley, retired health officer of three western states.

Liguori Publications has truly smoothed the way for *Dare to Commit* through all of its stages, beginning with Father Mathew Kessler, C.Ss.R., who was receptive to the subject when I proposed it. Christopher Orlet and especially Deborah Meister, my editors, took pains with the text and guided me through certain difficult passes. Christopher Miller has been my collaborator with the complex of permissions for multiple quotations. Finally, Liguori's Editorial Director, Jay Staten, had me write an article on this topic for the January 2010 issue of the *Liguorian* magazine. Thanks to these angel guardians.

****

Inc., New York/Mahwah, NJ. Reprinted by permission of Paulist Press, Inc. www.paulistpress.com

Excerpt from *Holy Listening: The Art of Spiritual Direction*, by Margaret Guenther. Cambridge, MA: Cowley, 1992. © 1992 Margaret Guenther.

Excerpt from *Homo Viator: Introduction to a Metaphysic of Hope*, by Gabriel Marcel, trans. by Emma Craufurd. Harper Torchbooks, 1962.

Excerpt from *Hybrid Cultures: Strategies for Entering and Leaving Modernity*, by Néstor García Canclini. Copyright © 1995 by the Regents of the University of Minnesota. Used by permission of University of Minnesota Press.

Excerpt from *Let Your Life Speak: Listening for the Voice of Vocation*, by Parker J. Palmer. San Francisco: Jossey-Bass, 2000. Copyright © 2000 by John Wiley & Sons, Inc.

Excerpt from Pope Benedict XVI, *Spe Salvi* (Encyclical Letter on Christian Hope), Nov. 30, 2007. © 2007 Libreria Editrice Vaticana.

Excerpt from *Priesthood Imperiled: A Critical Examination of Ministry in the Catholic Church*, by Bernard Häring, C.Ss.R. Liguori, MO: Triumph, 1996. © 1996 Bernard Häring. Used by permission.

Excerpts from *Rain of Gold* by Victor Villaseñor. NY: Dell Publishing, 1992. Copyright © 1991 by Victor Edmundo Villaseñor.

Excerpt from "Sex, Lies, and Hook-up Culture," an interview with Donna Freitas in *U.S. Catholic*, Nov. 2008. Used by permission of Claretian Publications.

Excerpt from "Teaching the Faith in a Postmodern World," by Carlo Maria Montini, in *America*, May 12, 2008. Used by permission of *America*.

Excerpt from *The Alchemist*, by Paulo Coelho. NY: Harper Collins, 1993. English version copyright © 1993 by Paulo Coelho and Alan R. Clarke.

Excerpt from *The Anatomy of Hope: How People Prevail in the Face of Illness*, by Jerome Groopman, M.D. NY: Random House, 2004. Copyright © 2004 by Jerome Groopman.

Excerpt from *The Christian Commitment: Essays in Pastoral Theology*, by Karl Rahner. Sheed and Ward, 1963.

Excerpt from a review of *The Lord of the Absurd* by Raymond J. Nogar, OP, reviewer D. A. Drennen, in *America*, Sept. 3, 1966. Used by permission of *America*.

Excerpts from "The Love Song of J. Alfred Prufrock" and "The Waste Land, V" in *COLLECTED POEMS* 1909-1962, by T. S. Eliot.

Excerpts from *The New Dictionary of Catholic Spirituality*, ed. Michael Downey, articles "Acedia" and "Discernment of Spirits." Copyright © 1993. Used by permission of The Liturgical Press, Collegeville, MN.

Excerpt from *THE ROAD LESS TRAVELED* by M. Scott Peck, MD (NY: Simon & Schuster, Inc., 1978). Used by permission.

Excerpts from *The Spiritual Exercises of Saint Ignatius: A Translation and Commentary*, by George E. Ganss, S.J. Copyright © 1992. Used by permission of The Institute of Jesuit Sources, St. Louis, MO.

Excerpt from *Wise Choices: A Spiritual Guide to Making Life's Decisions* by Margaret Silf, NY: Bluebridge, 2007. Text copyright © 2004, 2007 Margaret Silf.